Architecture
Design Made
Easy

WORKING DRAWINGS
FOR BEGINNERS

MGBEMENA Emeka Ebuz
OKONTA Ebere Donatus

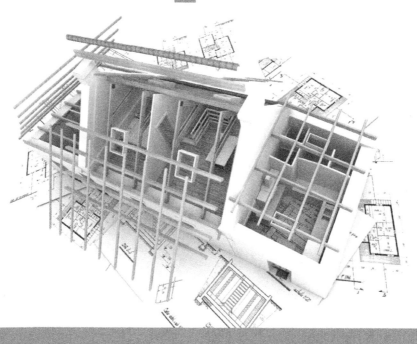

FOREWORD
Prof. JAIYEOBA Babatunde E.

ARCHITECTURE DESIGN MADE EASY

WORKING DRAWINGS FOR BEGINNERS

MGBEMENA, Emeka Ebuz

OKONTA, Ebere Donatus

Architecture Design Made Easy; Working Drawing for Beginners

Copyright © 2021 Mgbemena, E. E and Okonta, E. D.

ISBN:9798488348011

For further details, please contact:

The Authors,

Architecture Made Easy; Working Drawing for Beginners

Department of Architecture

Obafemi Awolowo University, Ile-Ife

P.M.B 13

Osun State. Nigeria

Requests for information should be addressed to:

Cover design: Ferricool Studios *(ferricoolcreativity@gmail.com)*

Table of Contents

vi

"Architects must be skillful with the pencil and have a knowledge of drawing so that he readily can make the drawings required to show the appearance of the work he proposes to construct" (Vitruvius Pollio, 1692).

DEDICATION

To all architecture students who have sought long for a clear path in the discipline, practice and profession of architecture.

ACKNOWLEDGEMENT

We are eternally indebted to individuals who in one way or the other supported, advised and inspired us during the course of writing this book.

We are grateful for the inspiration from Prof. and Prof. (Mrs.) S.A. Amole, Dr. A.O. Ilesanmi, Dr. P.S. Ogedengbe, Prof. and Dr. (Mrs.) Anyadike, Prof. E. Babatunde Jaiyeoba, Arc. Charles Onunze, Arc. Godspower Israel, thank you for all your support.

Thanks to Jessica Ghazi, Andrew Onyemenem, and Aideas studio for furnishing us with some of the drawings and basic information we need that simplified our discourse, we are really grateful for your kind gesture. We won`t forget to appreciate 'facetation' blog, whose records enable us to trace some timelines concerning the history of working drawings.

What can we do without families, who stood by our side through thick and thin, how much can we thank you enough for your constant and unwavering companionship and support? To Nkem and children, Grace Okonta, you are all much cherished.

Thanks to many other people who are too numerous to be mentioned, Staff, colleagues and friends from the University of Nigeria Nsukka (UNN), Enugu State, Abubakar Tafawa Balewa University (ATBU), Bauchi State, Obafemi Awolowo University (OAU), Ile-Ife, Osun State, who contributed directly or indirectly to this work. Thank you so very much.

To the publishers, Obafemi Awolowo University press limited for their tireless, consistent and passionate efforts towards the production of the book, we are grateful.

Finally, our utmost thanks to the Lord God Almighty, our personal bravery, and our invincible army; He makes our feet like hinds' feet and makes us walk, not to stand still in terror, but to walk and make spiritual progress upon our high places.

PREFACE

The problem facing architects in this twenty-first century, as far as design is concerned is basically the same as that which had confronted them throughout all ages because the basic principles of composition and drafting remain unchanged even though standards from place to place have been altered over time. Practical limitations, special requirements, local conditions produced in the design of the building are certain characteristics which may dominate most part of the design.

Working drawings are just a subset but a very important step in the entire design process. As such, architects must develop good design vocabularies in order to achieve an excellent result. Strict adherence to design rules and conventions will reduce the ambiguity created in most working drawings and enable architects to speak similar language over time, thus creating a clear pathway for other allied professionals to follow.

This book on working drawing will help to relay some of the dos and don'ts in drafting working drawings. It is good for practicing architects, students who are studying architecture or related courses, allied professionals and scholars.

It affords the reader the opportunity to reflect on the symbols, signs, explanations, terminologies that are likely to come up when preparing working drawings. It takes into consideration first-timers who have little or no experience in drafting skills; teaching from the rudimentary to the professional requirements.

It teaches students how to handle a complex network of lines representing various elements in the design, through the mastery of line prioritization.

This book, *Architecture Design Made Easy* specifically treated working drawings, cross-examining past works and clearly addressing issues that usually confront students. Subsequent volumes may delve into other aspects of architecture design that students find challenging.

No student of architecture remains the same when he or she has read this book. The positive change is dramatic. Thus, we humbly understand that we may still need to cross the `t`s and dot the `i`s and we sincerely welcome suggestions bearing in mind the next editions.

FOREWARD

In Architecture, graphic communication is as important as oral communication if not more important especially in the execution of design ideas. The ability to express ideas and concepts in drawings is one of the basic things an architecture student learns on admission to the school. The first stage is to learn freehand drawing and in contemporary times freehand drawing commences at the same time as digital communication with different 2D and 3D software. Freehand drawing and diverse software are now available for presentation drawings that are the first stage in translating the clients brief to discus-sable drawings.

Beyond the early years in school, architecture students get stock in this first stage of design idea communication known as presentation drawings, sketch design or schematic presentation. They get fascinated with the creative instinct of architects to evolve new ideas with the belief that other allied professionals in the building industry should resolve other details. Also, except for students that embark on compulsory or volunteer industrial attachment with professionals on the field, progressing to working drawings has been difficult. Many students lack the industrial exposure and the on-site experience necessary for the knowledge in working drawings preparation. Working drawings as the major means of communicating ideas of design from the designer to the client(s) organization, other consultants, approval authorities, the executor/contractor and any other party to the contract is necessarily based on knowledge of materials, construction methods and behaviour of materials in different loading conditions and structural concepts is an uphill task for students in training. Meanwhile, architects and architectural firms in practice who are prospective employers of the fresh graduates expect them to be skilled in both presentation and working drawings.

The authors- Mgbemena and Okonta, decided to alleviate the problem for architects in training through this publication on working drawings. Architecture though as old as man is one of the later disciplines in academia. It is even much younger in Nigeria where the Nigeria Institute of Architects was formed in 1960 by the first generation of Architects mostly trained outside the country and the regulatory body- Architects Registration Council of Nigeria (ARCON)- was only empowered through a decree in 1969. The first university-based architecture programme in Nigeria only started in 1962. Therefore and because of many other inhibiting factors, there are very few architecture books written in Nigeria. This is why the bold initiative of the authors should be appreciated and applauded. However, working drawing as a mode of communication is evolving and it is only an input in many transformations on-going in the project delivery process like Building Information Modelling (BIM), Virtual Reality (VR), Augmented Reality (AR) and Internet of Things (IoT). Many editions of this book are therefore expected to improve and upgrade the information as transformations take place, this is a challenge to the authors.

The book is a good introduction to working drawings for beginners who seek to have inroads to the basics of working drawings preparation.

Prof E. Babatunde JAIYEOBA PhD

July, 2019.

Chapter One

INTRODUCTION

1.0   Drawing and Types of Drawing

Seated in the very heart of every man[1] is the deep and passionate desire to be heard and understood by another. From the little child who is less than a year old to the Chief Executive Officer (CEO) of a company, is the desire to communicate his thoughts clearly so as to convey a message to others. Man can go to any length just to convey his ideas, no wonder some companies spend millions of naira to advertise in the Cable Network News (CNN) for just a few seconds; this in itself speaks volumes, that is, oftentimes there is a price to pay just to get others to understand what we are saying. The medium of expression goes a long way to show the kind of audience we will have and how they will understand what we want to put across to them.

Thus, man seeks to satisfy this pure craving by communicating his thoughts and feelings through the various forms of visual art like sculpture, design, crafts, painting, drawing, ceramics, photography, video, film-making and architecture besides written communication.

---

[1] Man, in this context is a generic term

Drawing as part of this visual art is the oldest form of communication by which man makes use of various tools (drawing media[2] and/or digital tools) and techniques[3] to express his thoughts, feelings and way of channeling his creative initiative by way of visible markings done on a surface.[4]

The `beautiful` truth about all forms of visual art is that there is a link or relationship between them, and this makes it difficult to exclusively isolate one from the other. Architecture itself over the years cannot be isolated from either painting, ceramics, photography, crafts, and more. The practice of drawing is not confined purely to the field of arts, it has been used effusively in the fields of science and social science for which architecture both as a science and an art is not excluded. Hence, in the fields of science, social science and arts exist numerous types of drawings which fall under the two major categories of drawing; drawings that seek to express some degree of realism in representation and those that utilize conventions to render representations that are artificial or unnatural as classified below:

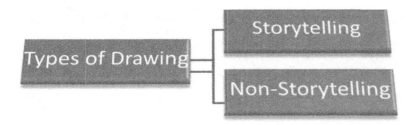

Figure 1 Type of Drawings

---

[2] These include pen and ink, charcoals, crayons, pastels, markers, graphite and wax colour pencils etc. Digital tools can also inspire the effect of these dry medias
[3] Examples are hatching, stippling, blending, cross hatching, line drawing.
[4] Surface like paper, cardboard, plastic, walls, floors, plastic, leather, canvas etc.

Those that fall in the categories of Storytelling include the following;

- Anime
- Comics
- Cartoons

Those that fall in the categories of Non-Storytelling include the following;

- Stick Figure
- Silhouette
- Figure Drawing
- Caricature
- Gesture Drawing
- Portrait
- Sketch: (Croquis, Doodle, Study, Scribble and so on)
- Technical Drawing (**Architectural drawing,** Electrical drawing, Structural drawing, Scientific and Archaeological illustration, plumbing drawing) and so on

The non-storytelling type of drawing contains the category of drawing for which we will consider architectural drawings and narrow it down to working drawings.

Types Of Architectural Drawings

The major types of drawings that are related to architectural drawing types are listed below (though not exclusively only these).

- Presentation Drawings
- Survey Drawings
- Record Drawings

- Working Drawings (Production drawings)

Presentation Drawings: These are drawings that are intended to appear realistic but do not carry sufficient details intended for the execution of building projects on site. They are similar in style to working drawings made to communicate design concepts or proposals and may often contain basically anthropometric features like trees, shrubs, people, vehicles, sculptors, et cetera. Architects can produce this type of drawing with the help of a graphic designer, employing the use of manual or electronic means for editing and productions.

Figure 2: A 3D view of a Living Area (showing various elements that beautify it)

Source: Aideas Studioz

Figure. 3: A 3D view of a mixed-use building

Source: Aideas Studioz

Survey Drawings: Though often produced by a Land Surveyor, it is a type of drawing that shows exact and accurate dimensions of existing land, structure(s) and building(s) which forms the bases of an architect`s working drawing and gives breath to it. Other times, they show terrain, nearby structures, waterbody, etc.

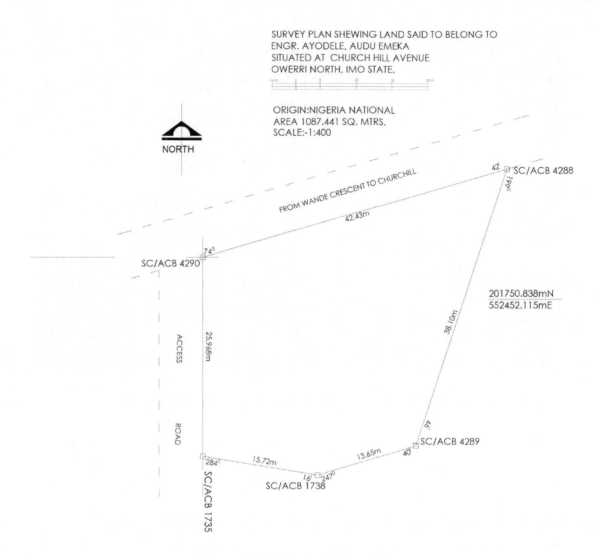

Figure 4: A Simple Survey Plan

Record Drawings (Constructed Drawings): To clearly understand what record drawings are, it is expedient that clarifications are made with regards to *'as-built drawings'*, *'record drawings'* and *'measured drawings'*.

22

It is often the practice for minor or considerable changes to be made for several reasons. When such changes are made, the client may require that as-built drawings (drawings that reflect those changes and shows what has been built) are produced during construction or at the completion of construction. The contractor is saddled with the task to 'mark-up' to the final construction issue drawings on-site using red ink, *such changes done by the contractor to the original design are referred to as, **as-built drawings** (that is, what was actually built by the contractor)*. The as-built drawings may risk liability since they are variations from the original design.

When the contractor makes such changes on the original documents and drawings (approved by addendum or clarification by the architect and approved by the owner), it is used by the architect and his team to prepare a final compiled drawing called, **'record drawings'** that show the completed project. The record drawing is more reliable than the as-built drawing because it has been scrutinized and approved by the architect.

While the **'measured drawings'** are prepared during the process of undertaking renovation or documentation of an existing building. They are prepared from the measurements, details and specifications gotten from an existing building or from on-site project data.

Working Drawings: It is sometimes referred to as production drawings are sets of drawings produced by the architect in the second phase (pre-contract stage) of normal architectural service, which assist the builder(s) in erecting the structure. (Thomas, 1978) defined working drawings as a communication medium used to graphically convey the design requirements for a construction project. Working Drawings are used for tendering, contract document, base information, statutory approvals, developing as-built drawings, developing construction programme, review/feedback source.

1.1   Brief History of Architectural Working Drawings

To explore the history of working drawings is to learn more about architecture itself, for they are inseparable. There is no number of pages sufficient to discuss down memory lane the history of working drawings however, emphasis will be made on certain timelines. This emphasis on the outline may not be comprehensive enough but it conveys some basics.

Classic Era (850BC to 476 AD)

Let's begin with the words of the great architect Vitruvius, he said, "architects must be skillful with the pencil and have a knowledge of drawing so that he readily can make the drawings required to show the appearance of the work he proposes to construct" (Vitruvius & Morgan, 1960). Although, later years to come suggest that man should not be ready with those manual drafting tools but digital tools too. However, thousands of years before the paper was invented, Gudea, the Chaldean Engineer made an inscription on a stone tablet that depicted the floor plan of a fortress that was as far back as 2130 BC (Gieseke, Mitcell, & Spencer, 1974). The common practice in those days was to use other kinds of surfaces such as stones for inscriptions.

However, Vitruvius In Book 1.2 of De Architectura Vitruvius recommended that architects should adopt three kinds of architectural presentations or ideas.

They include:

- ichnographia, or the ground plan,
- orthographia, or the vertical frontal image, and
- scaenographia. (though interpreted by some authors to mean section while others perspective) Vitruvius & Morgan, 1960.

In spite of the above, the use of images was not universally endorsed in the ancient world for several reasons which cut across copyrights for those images, but that did not deter Romans who developed many drawings and surveying instruments such as A-level and the compass (Booker and Parsons 1968). Most of the builders of early cathedrals borrowed many construction techniques from the Romans who built their buildings essentially by slave labour. The beginning of the medieval periods saw the emergence of craftsmen's masons who had undergone an apprenticeship process and were given responsibilities to design or construct buildings.

Gothic Era (110 to 1450 AD)

Those mansons maintained personal sketchbooks and lodge books, but there is no record of whether they used them for construction. Most cathedrals then were designed without the help of drawings. But, a good example of some sketches is that of Villard de Honnecourt dating from about 1040 CE who through his sketches annotated in Latin, demonstrated common building techniques from the world of cathedral construction showing sketches of rose windows, partial elevations of existing cathedrals, statute and pulpits. Though most masons lacked formal education or advanced linguistic ability, their drawings were not dimensioned or detailed but a means of distributing knowledge both within a specific construction site and between sites.

The masons[5] also developed geometrical techniques that could be learned by rote and be used to develop vaults and other structural forms using simple Euclidean shapes (Shelby 1964; 1972).

The design drawings of the Masons were highly abstract geometrical shapes that could be used to lay out ceiling arches and groins, for the mason relied on their own documentary conventions for constructions. Those shapes were either primarily rotated or transformed. The shapes were transcribed from either lodge books or memory onto a sketching floor where they could be geometrically scaled to the suitable size for construction (in this case a cathedral). These drawings lacked annotations and were hard to interpret.

The study of medieval drawings has proven over the years to be intricate, there are several postulated reasons for this, however, Harvey, 1972) explained the main reason why few drawings yet exist. He had two explanations for this: The first explanation concerns the ephemeral nature of architectural drawings. The value of buildings arguably lies in the building itself rather than the documents that were used to construct it. Many intact drawings survived because they were completely forgotten in an obscure location rather than through any sort of veneration. Other drawing fragments exist because the initial heavy parchment documents were cut up and used to bind other texts. The second explanation concerns the content of the documents. The secrecy of the masons is well known and it is not unlikely that they destroyed documents that could lead to an erosion of their craft. In one extreme case, a mason reportedly killed a bishop who had learned the secret of waterproofing foundations! (Harvey, 1972) But that did not shrug the fact that many categories of drawings still existed and many principles were expressed

---

[5] Mason is a skilled worker who builds or works with stone, brick or concrete. The word 'mason' was first used in the Middle Age, in the 13th Century, also referred to as a craftsman

which were to become a baseline for subsequent Renaissance. For example;

Draw simply, but in a concentrated manner. Try hard to manage with one sheet of paper for each device but, avoid mere hints that might possibly confuse a less skilled beholder. Therefore, draw all particular details distinctly; if necessary, enlarge items that might help to understand the function. Spare your distant colleagues the rigour of having to work out his own solutions for a result you have already achieved.

Do without multiple viewpoints but, pay extreme attention to the one you ultimately choose. Move laterally and upward until the maximum is visible and be a minimum concealed.

If elements decisive for the function cannot be shown in a general view, then separate them from the context. Draw them enlarged next to their correct position. Form a pictorial "subordinate clause" and join it with a "conjunction" in the form of notes or lines to the "main clause." If such a separately rendered part or mechanism is applied in several sketches, a brief indication will suffice in the following pages.

If the machine is so complicated that too many parts will remain hidden and too many necessary pictorial "subordinate clauses" will obscure the whole context, then restructure "the text". Make a series of new "main clauses". Show all parts separately and connect them again by adding a general view in order to enable the beholder to discern their relationship.

If you are dealing with such an extended ensemble of mechanisms and machines that all single elements would result in an unfathomable puzzle of sketches, then exploit all your pictorial resources of analysis, segmentation, and structuring. Form a "text." Tell a story. Present a general view as introduction and orientation. Then hold on to sequences of shafts, forces, and functions. There you may fix other "subordinate clauses" until the whole pictorial "text" fits together seamlessly in your beholder's mind. (Leng, 2004, pp.104-105)

Renaissance Period (1400 to 1600 AD)

Referred to as the 'age of awakening' in Italy, France, and England. The rediscovery of Paolo Uccello`s perspective, Leonardo da Vinci`s copious sketchbooks showing exploded views, assembly drawings and detailed cutaways, the works of Albrecht Dürer, Francesco di Georgio Martini are just a few popular works of the renaissance period. But in spite of the great skill displayed by Leonardo and Dürer, their works still lacked some features like dimensioning and tolerancing. Indeed, Dürer explained that the actual construction of structures required two things: a wooden model which enabled the workers to visualize the structure in three dimensions and the use of a working drawing or tracing floor where designs could be transcribed at a 1:1 scale (Camerota, 2004).

In spite of the increasing drawings of perspective in this period, it was yet frowned at. As a matter of fact, Baldassare Castiglione and Raphael wrote to Pope Leo X around 1519 and indicated that plan, elevation, and section are far more important than perspective when generating illustrations of ancient ruins.

It was during the Renaissance that formal training in drawing techniques was initiated. Venice's Accademia, Del Disegno was established in 1543 as a way of training painters, sculptors, and architects in standard practices. The Accademia stood in marked contrast to the then-dominant closed training of the guilds (Henninger-Voss, 2004).

Henninger-Voss (2004, pg. 155) notes: "*Measured design was the bond between the experience of the engineer and his pretensions to science. It was also the chain of good faith that bound the lieutenants, commanders, junior and senior engineers, and the counsels of government. It was the means by which decisions that could affect the lives of hundreds of men, or thousands of people, could be made at a distance of hundreds of miles. It is no coincidence that military engineers tried to impress on their patrons the epistemological foundation of their practice—not merely for rhetorical effect, but often in conscientious earnestness.*"

During the Renaissance, architectural drawings began to conform with their modern appearance of particular importance to architects, was the rediscovery of the architectural works of Vitruvius, combined with that of linear perspective, of particular importance were the three representation views: ichnographia (ground plan), orthographia, (vertical frontal image), and scaenographia (either section or perspective).

Modern Times

Until the mid-19th century, Architects relied on skilled Draftsmen to faithfully copy their sketches or drawings for the purpose of distribution. The Draftsmen's men used tools like the set-squares, compass, dividers, tee squares, stencils, French curves, scale rules and more.

Working drawings have come to be thoroughly improved but not before the blueprinting technology, which was introduced in 1842. The blueprinting is a process where the architectural drawing was reproduced on a semi-transparent paper, then weighted down on top of a sheet of paper or cloth that was coated with a photosensitive chemical mixture of potassium ferricyanide and ferric ammonium citrate. After it is done, it is then exposed to light. The exposed parts of the drawing that is, the background became blue, while the drawing lines blocked the coated paper from exposure and remained white. With the dawn of blueprints, multiple copies and individual 'detail' or 'bench' drawings could be made for each component. After the blueprints were introduced, labourers were now required to clearly follow the requirements of the drawing and use only the dimensions explicitly rendered by the designer. Several transitions and modifications occurred even with the use of the blueprint technology and that ushered in the modern technology that aided drafting and processing drawings for construction processes. But that soon changed when the photocopiers were introduced that made the duplication of drawings easier and faster.

However, the most evident changes are the introduction of Computer-Aided Design (CAD) technology, which came towards the end of the 20th century and brought about revolutions in drafting working drawings. The first of such technology can be traced to the year 1957 when Dr. Patrick J. Hanratty developed PRONTO (Program for Numerical Tooling Operations) which was a commercial numerical-control programming system and first of its kind but, five years later Ivan Sutherland, a Ph.D. student in Massachusetts Institute of Technology (MIT) in his thesis created the 'Sketchpad' a Graphic User Interface (GUI) to generate X-Y plots. The organizational innovation used in 'Sketchpad' initiated the use of object-oriented programming in modern CAD.

The 1960s was a year booming with inventions as it pertains to CAD. This includes the developments of the first digitizer (from Auto-trol) and DAC-1 and several companies were funded to commercialize their CAD programs. All these were in the bid to improve 2D drafting techniques, but the stage was being set for 3D drawings. The first of such was the work of Ken Versprillle in the 1970s whose discoveries of NURBS for his Ph.D. thesis formed the basis of modern 3D curve and surface modeling. But the work of the Hungarian scientist named Gabor Bajor cannot be written off as he took a great risk to smuggle Macintosh computers into his communist-controlled homeland with the intent of writing a 3D CAD program. He succeeded in creating the program and began the Graphsoft company. In 1985, Diehl Graphsoft launched MiniCAD and that same year Autodesk invented AutoCAD 2.1 which was complete with 3D capabilities.

These inventions greatly improved digital drafting techniques and CAD has continued ever since to mark huge milestones in its evolution with superb improvements. Today, there are tons of CAD software's widely used for architectural working drawings especially with the world of BIM, one can only imagine and it may be true what the future of CAD software's and the massive improvements it will bring to working drawings,

1.2   Architectural Working Drawings

In order to erect any structure, working drawings must be produced stating in clear terms the sizes, materials and configuration of the various elements. This need for working drawing forms the foundation for any construction work. Such information like the basic dimensions, space sizes, location of structural and non-structural elements (columns, walls, beams, arches, girders) are the basis for doing a working drawing.

Success in Architecture and Engineering fields requires a high degree of proficiency in working drawing preparation.

Working Drawings are sets of drawings produced by the architect in the second phase (pre-contract stage) of normal architectural service, which assist the builder(s) in erecting the structure. Thomas, M.L (1978) defined working drawings as a communication medium that aims to graphically convey the design requirements for a construction project. The emphasis should be on clear communication with minimum use of lines and words. This can only be possible if the drafter has a high knowledge of the drafting technique. Working drawings are not a time for rendering. The drafter should use the simplest methods, lines, conventional signs, and recognizable forms to drive home his or her message. It is the final stage in the drawing process unless there are corrections, additions or subtraction during the contract stage, which may be treated as variations or additional work as the case may be.

In general, the drawings communicate in visual terms the purpose; the notes, numbers and names explain it and the title panel identifies it. Other professionals like engineers, surveyors, planners and specialty contractors may be required at some point in the pre-contract and contract stage to produce similar drawings. Structural, mechanical, electrical and interior design drawings can be produced concurrently with the architectural working drawings. Working drawings are used for planning approval, construction works, for use by other consultants, for preparing the tender documents, for litigation and arbitration purposes, for inspection and monitoring and maintenance. The type of project determines whether the architectural drawings are the prime drawings from where other professionals draw inspiration or not.

Working drawings are subdivided into three:

- Location Drawings
- Assembly Drawings
- Component Drawing

Location Drawings: These are drawings that show 'WHERE' the construction elements are located and are often referred to as general arrangement drawings. They include plans, sections and elevations.

For example, from Figure 5a below the floor plan drawing (part of general arrangement drawing) is meant to show the location of a standard flush door. This example will enable us to understand the components and assembly drawings.

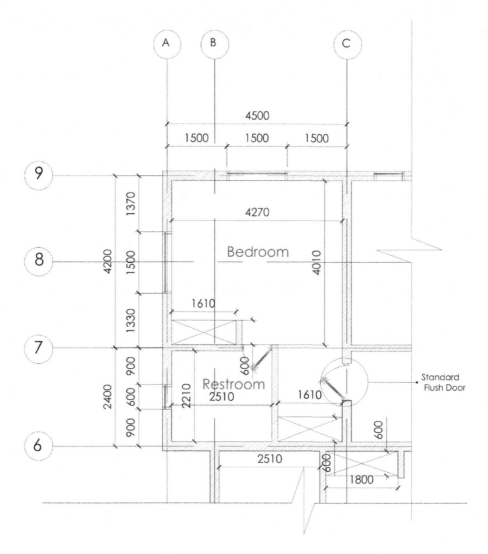

Figure 5a: Partial Floor Plan showing the location of a door (a smaller component)

Assembly Drawings: These drawings represent the relationship between components and show 'HOW' different parts and components fit together. They are used to represent items that consist of more than one component. Assembly drawings are often shown on the general arrangement drawing or in some cases detail drawings. Often times they include instructions, lists of component parts, reference numbers, references to detail drawings or shop drawings and most importantly specification information.

In the figure below, section B-B gives a clear picture of the assembly aspect of the drawing.

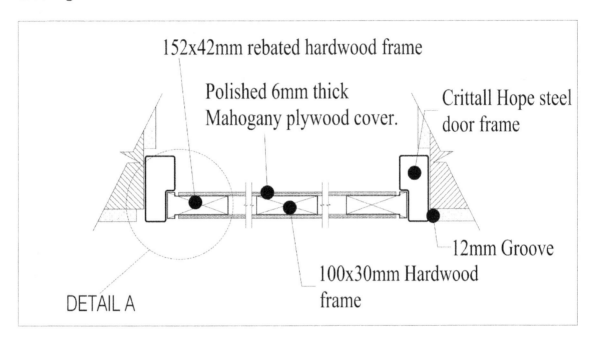

152x42mm rebated hardwood frame

Polished 6mm thick
Mahogany plywood cover.

Crittall Hope steel
door frame

12mm Groove

100x30mm Hardwood
frame

DETAIL A

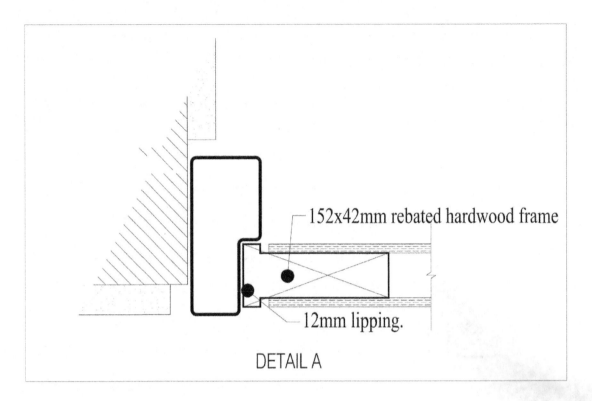

Figure 5b: Assembly Drawing; showing how the part fit together (See detail A)

Component Drawing: These are drawings that show 'WHAT' the component is and its characteristics. They are often 'self-contained' and may be obtained from a single supplier. There are times the combination of a component may be described as an 'assembly'. Component drawings can be categorized into two; smaller components (windows, beams, doors, coping stone, sills and so on) and larger components (roof trusses, cladding, cupboards and kitchens). When component drawings are drawn, they include information or references to the relevant parts providing useful information about materials, minimum quality, dimensions and detailed information are found in the specification document.

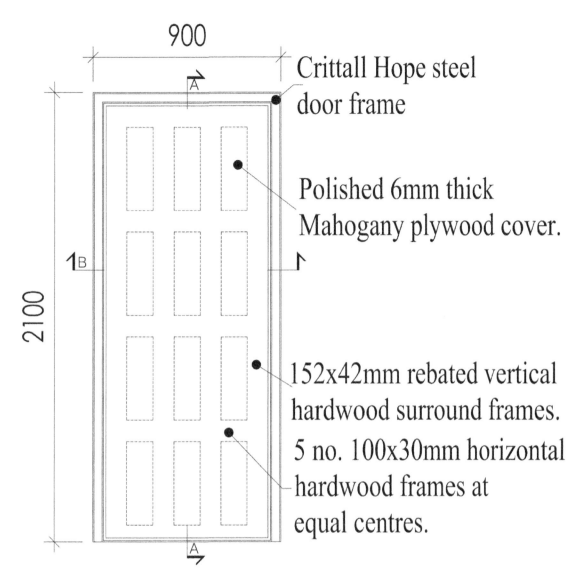

900

2100

Crittall Hope steel
door frame

Polished 6mm thick
Mahogany plywood cover.

152x42mm rebated vertical
hardwood surround frames.

5 no. 100x30mm horizontal
hardwood frames at
equal centres.

Figure 5c: Component (Flush Door)

Though, the flush door gives details of the characteristics of the component, the standard practice for such major details to be contained in the detail section of the drawing, schedules and specification documents.

A working drawing will not be said to be complete, comprehensive and useable for various purposes of construction if it does not reflect on these three subdivisions.

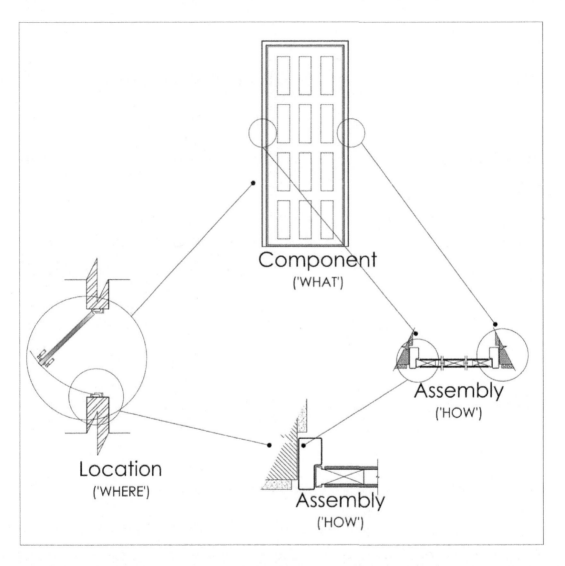

Figure 5d: Showing how the location, component and assembly drawing integrate together

In working drawing, every other information is generated from these three above, any student of architecture who understands these elements properly will not have a problem producing a comprehensive set of drawings. The ambiguity and lack of sufficient information for working drawing as seen in the details, specification and schedules is the lack of detailed production drawing, rooted in the misunderstanding of location, assembly and component drawing. No complete working drawing exist without reflecting these three, every other allied profession like structural or mechanical engineers' drawings are incomplete without these three, they give breath to every working drawing.

1.4 Evaluation of Tools And Software's For Working Drawings Production

Media[6] refers to both the material that is manually applied and to the base onto which it is applied (Mayer 1940). Quality tools and its comprehensive understanding will enhance the efficiency of drafting working drawings. The focus will be to consider *the drawing media*, *drawing equipment and tools* and *drawing base or surface* in two categories.

- Manual and Mechanical Drafting Methods
- Electronic (digital) Drafting Methods (CAD[7])

---

[6] That is, Drawing Media
[7] Computer-Aided Design

Manual and Mechanical Drafting Methods:

Practically, manual drafting is still essential and accessible in the 21st century. As a matter of fact, the practice in most architectural schools in Nigeria and beyond encourage the concept that a certain percentage of studio drawings for students be produced manually. As much as we are flooded with digital methods of drafting in the 21st century and most of the working drawings produced for construction purposes are done using CAD, and will still be in the next century, does not mean that architects-in-training should not be groomed in the discipline and practice of using manual methods to produce working drawings. If architectural education will be preserved to the next generation, then it must concern itself with exploring other means of understanding through diverse methods of which manual drafting should be inclusive. It is difficult to find a good architect who has not learned the mastery of using a pencil to communicate his thoughts. Often times, some of the great building design concepts started with the Architect scribbling down, using any of the drawing media (dry or wet) to express his thoughts. It helps the architect to form ideas since design software is more suited for precision.

Manual drafting is practical and experimental (helps a student understand the intricacies of buildings and their components), the development of CAD stemmed from the understanding of the manual methods of drafting. It is the fastest way any student of architecture can learn about the basics of certain drawing elements like line weights and its usage, understand how projected drawings (perspective, axonometric) work. Truly speaking, manual drafting helps ideas come out of the head easier and faster and there is a 'romance, emotion and pleasure' that sketching brings.

Back to evaluating these manual drafting methods, which we will highlight under these headings:

- *the drawing media,*
- *drawing equipment and tools* and
- *drawing base or surface*

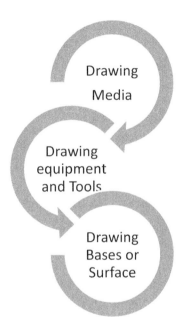

Figure 6: Category for manual drafting

Drawing Media: This can be grouped into dry media and wet media

- **Dry Media**: Graphite (pencil lead), charcoal, pastels, Conte, silverpoint, crayon
- **Wet media**: cartridge pens, inks (water-based, Indian/Chinese ink), rapidograph, and watercolor.

Pencils come with graphite[8]. This graphite is in several grades, those that are relatively hard and soft (contains lower proportions of clay).

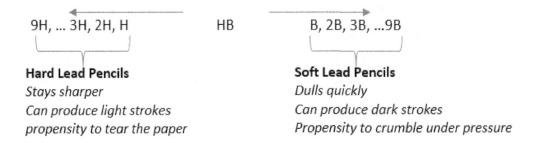

9H, … 3H, 2H, H   HB   B, 2B, 3B, …9B

Hard Lead Pencils
Stays sharper
Can produce light strokes
propensity to tear the paper

Soft Lead Pencils
Dulls quickly
Can produce dark strokes
Propensity to crumble under pressure

Figure 7: Graphite grading scales and properties

The grade B pencils are especially useful in rendering and sketching, while the grade H pencils can help with construction lines, architectural line works, etc.

Graphite lead (in different scales) also are used in mechanical pencils often referred to as 'clutch pencils' (the common clutch pencil points are in 0.5mm, 0.3mm or 0.7mm point)

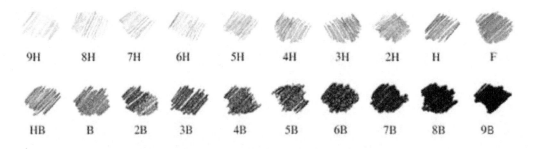

9H   8H   7H   6H   5H   4H   3H   2H   H   F

HB   B   2B   3B   4B   5B   6B   7B   8B   9B

Figure 8: Graphite Grading Scales and Properties

---

[8] A silvery-gray form of carbon

N: B the letter 'F' indicates that the pencil sharpens to a fine point.

Though in digital methods of drafting for example, in AutoCAD these pencil points are replaced with the 'layer' icon with several improved options.

The understanding of the different grades of pencil helps in drawing lines and representing line weights in terms of the pressure applied on the surface of the drawing or the pencil`s graphite scale. One cannot use a 2B pencil to draw construction lines or draw hidden details because that will be a wrong application.

The technical pens have proved to be an efficient tool for many drafters because it helps in producing consistent lines of the same thickness as long as they are infilled with ink, they come in the range of 0.1mm -2.0mm. The common brands include Rotring, Staedler, Faber Castle. It can be used to reproduce drawings on tracing papers.

Drawing Equipment's and Tools

A tool is any device that simplifies work or plays a vital role in the performance of a task. The following are an example of combinations of tools and equipment that can be used in working drawing production.

- **Drawing/Drafting Boards**

This can be made of several materials including wood, high resin particle board, tempered hardboard, etc. For some, the surface is coated with melamine so that the surface is smooth, free from bumps and provides durability. Drawing boards help a great deal to ensure some level of accuracy, comfort, consistency, etc. They come in different sizes (A0, A1, A2 and A3) and types. The drawing board can be adjusted in height to suit the user and tilted to desired angles but, care must be taken for the surface to still accommodate other drawing instruments like the set-squares or the Tee Square. Below are some fine examples of modern drawing boards.

Figure 9: Drafting Table with under desktop storage shelf and padded stool

Source: amazon.com

Figure 10. A Drafting Table fitted with a lamp

Source: haocai.us

The portable size drawing boards make drawing in the outdoors quite easy and the board can be carried easily compared to the other types.

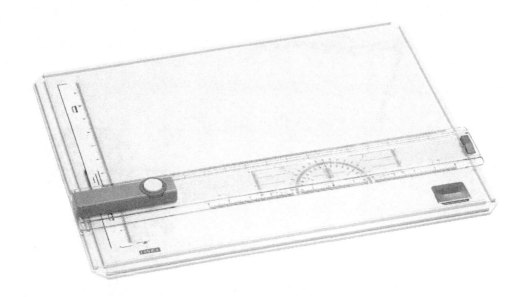

Figure 11. Portable A3 size drawing board

Source: yaltalibraua.com

- **Scale Rules:** Helps in the basic reduction in sizes, such as 1:10, 1:100, or 1:200. Examples include the architects scales, engineers scales, metric scales, etc.

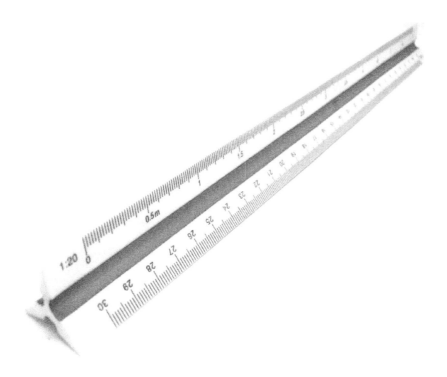

Figure 12: Scale rule

Source: textbookcentre.com

- **Set-squares:** They come in two forms as can be seen in Figure 13 below. They are used to draw parallel and perpendicular lines and some measured angles (45^0 60^0 30^0); combining it with the tee square can make for a more excellent production. The adjustable set squares make the drawing of angles flexible and easy.

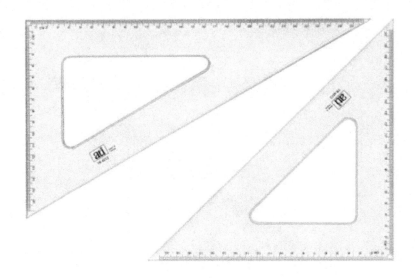

Figure 13: Two types of set-squares (45-degree (left) and 30/60-degree (right) angles)

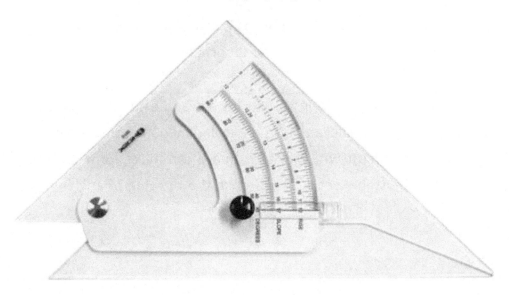

Figure 14: Adjustable Setsquares
Source: draftex.com.au

- **T-Squares**

They help in drawing horizontal lines on a drawing table and may be useful to set the drawing paper on the drawing board and excellently used with set squares to guide vertical and diagonal lines. There are different sizes (460mm, 610mm, 760mm, etc.) and types of tee- squares made from stainless steel, wood and plastic. The head of the tee- square can be made to be permanent, movable or adjustable. Though they are all excellent although the transparent type may offer great visibility across the drawing surface.

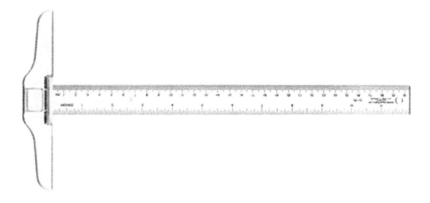

Figure 15 A Tee Square

Source: joann.com

- **Templates**

They are used for drawing standard symbols, including lettering, mechanical, circles, ellipses, flowchart, human figure template, traffic templates, etc.

Circle templates: This type of template is based on fractions and multiples of an inch with different series of circles. For circles ranging from 1-36mm.

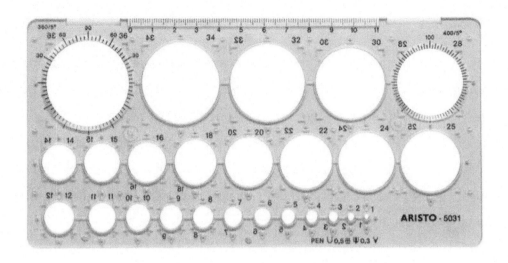

Figure 16: Circle Template

Source: imaginationinternationalinc.com

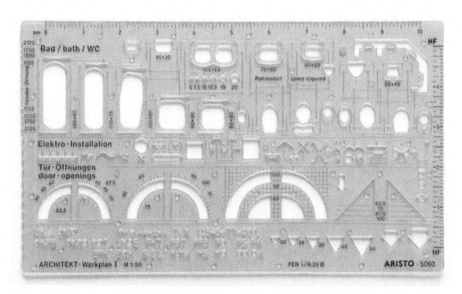

Figure17: Architectural Template

Source: imaginationinternationalinc.com

Figure 18 Radius Template

Source: imaginationinternationalinc.com

- **Lettering Stencil:** A guide used in drafting to produce letters. It comes in different scales and types. It is particularly useful because of the consistency it brings.

Figure 19: Lettering Stencil

Source: wikiwand.com

Other drawing tools include the following:

- Protractor
- Dividers
- Drafting tape, masking tape, stainless steel clips to affix the sheets to the board
- Pencil sharpeners: This gives sharp angles to the tip of the pencils.
- Craft knives or scalpels can be used to sharpen a pencil
- Erasers
- Correction fluids
- French Curve
- Ruler
- Steel rules: used repeatedly to draw lines
- Compasses and so on.

Drawing Base Or Surface: Unlike the ancient times, some of the bases encircle around the walls, metal, canvas, plaster, metal, walls-typically for murals, wood, etc., though much more recently, working drawings have been produced on paper which could be opaque or translucent in this case a drawing paper or a tracing paper respectively. The tracing paper has a great advantage over the paper in the sense that it can accept ink to a great extent compared to the paper. Even though the grade of paper determines how much ink it can accept on its surface. Thus, it is the practice in most schools to train students to use the tracing paper to communicate their ideas.

- **Drawing paper Sizes**

The drawing paper comes in different sizes and standards. They exist in series, that is, A Series, B-Series, and C-series. The A-Series drawing paper size (defined by ISO[9] 216 standard) is the most widely accepted standard used for all drawings, printed sheets and written materials. For whichever size that must be used, standard practice demand that the surface is free of every particle or dirt.

The paper as a base for drawing is paramount, oftentimes it is advisable that the same type of sheet is used throughout the drawings to maintain consistency. There are the A, B and C series with different sizes.

DESIGNATION	DIMENSIONS
A0	841MM x 1189mm
A1	594mm x 841mm
A2	420mm x 594mm
A4	210mm x 297mm
A5	149mm x 210mm

Table 1: Regular Dimension Sheet

Until relatively recently, this was the only available method.

---

[9] International Standard Organization

Drawing Techniques

- Automatic Drawing
- Blind Contour Drawing
- Contour Drawing
- Chiaroscuro Drawing
- Grisaille
- Hatching
- Masking
- Stippling
- Trois Crayons (Using three colours, typically black, white and sanguine chalks)
- Drybrush and so on

Electronic (digital) Drafting Methods (CAD)

Working drawings can be produced electronically (on a computer screen using a mouse and printing the result), with the use of computer-aided design software's to produce 2D drawings and 3D models. It is required that the Architect be trained to use the drafting tools. Some of the software's share similar concepts in usage but may be quite different in application. Hence, though like someone said, '*to know the heart of a sorcerer is to know them all',* in this case it is quite different, the knowledge of a particular software does not substitute for another, even though it may help, it is required that the designer or architect be trained to use the software.

We want to say it is a misconception to say that the 'emergence' CAD came to replace manual drafting technique, which will be an aberration in our view and will make a mess of the philosophy that most architectural schools tend to inculcate in students, which may have far-reaching consequences. We will like to think that CAD complements the manual method of drafting and not in any case meant to replace it.

However, since the inception of CAD for more than 50 years ago, it has been of great benefits and has greatly improved the design and construction of buildings across the globe, some of those benefits include:

- Storage, editing and modifications of drawings made easy
- Very accurate designs can be produced and simulated
- Saves time and considerable efforts employed in building design
- Creating superb documentations of the designs
- Enabling the architect or designer to visualize the design and its integral parts before its construction
- It enables conformity to industry and company standards
- Drawings can be printed on different scales, shared and the resolutions can be changed, and so on.

Though CAD still has some of its cons, for example, it requires training and usage to master a particular software (even though every new release needs the user to update his skills) some of those training may have some cost implications. For example, if the system crashes all works can be lost, and some of the software is quite expensive for a student or an architect-in-training to purchase.

N: B A quick look at some of the CAD software's that can be used for working drawing productions is seen in table 2, it is not a comprehensive table, and we are not seeking to exalt any software above another for they are all useful in design, though with striking peculiarities but what you will see in the table is just a piece of information that in an abridged way sheds a bit of light on the software itself. Some of the information relayed was gotten directly from the websites which are referenced in the third column. Other important information pertaining to the cost of the software, basic tutorial options and other product details can be obtained from the website.

SOFTWARE	DESCRIPTION	FEATURES
AutoCAD Architecture	First released in 1982 by Autodesk, is one of the most widely used 2D and 3D software's by architects and other allied professionals (MEP engineers, industrialist, and graphic designers)	*Compatible with other Softwares *Available in different languages *Enable topnotch documentation (editing live sections, room documentation, annotation and scaling, etc.) *Customization (layer-based order display, easy style access, etc.) *Intuitive user-interface that comes with built-in design layouts *Provides analytical tools for professionals to analyze building components and troubleshoot the stress and load levels of every support structure of a virtually designed building Reference:www.autodesk.com/products/autocad-architecture/overview
AUTODESK REVIT Revit Architecture	A design software built specifically for Building Information Modelling (BIM) it includes several features for architectural design, MEP Structural	*Collaborate: multiple project contributors can access centrally shared models and helps reduce clashes and rework *Visualize: communicate design intent more effectively to project owners and team members by

	engineering, and construction	using models to create high-impact 3D visuals *Design: model building components, analyze and simulate systems and structures, and iterate designs. Generate documentation from models *Detect clashes in aggregated models and identify costly conflicts *Reference:* *www.autodesk.com/products/revit-family/overview*
GRAPHISOFT. ARCHICAD	A 2D and 3D modeling design software developed by Graphisoft® launched in 1987 but founded in 1982. It allows for architectural rendering and visualization.	*BIM Design tool and curriculum implementation *Allows for the import and export of DWG, DXF and IFC and BCF files among others *Allows users to work with parametric objects *Model-based Team Collaboration Element association to story heights: Enables designers certain building elements (walls, column) to stories in an architectural manner. *Reference:* *www.myarchicad.com*

Chief Architect	A privately-owned top-rated home design software for architects, interior designers, etc. Released in 1992 and owned by a software developer in Coeur d` Alene, Idaho, United States.	*Instant materials list and schedules to cost jobs *Creates professional residential construction drawings for permits, subcontractors and clients *Enables realistic renderings, 360^0 renderings, live 3D viewer models and virtual tours *Compatible with AutoCAD and allows the import of PDF files, SketchUp 8 object, image files (BMP, JPG, PCS, TIFF, PCX, PNG, Metafiles, TGA) *Reference: www.chiefarchitect.com*
SketchUp	Founded in 2000 and developed by Trimble Inc. Design software that can be used by architects, interior designers, civil mechanical engineers, etc. for 3D modeling.	*Produced scaled, accurate drawings *Generate presentation documents *Intuitive Design, Documentation, vector drawing and communication *Animated walkthroughs creation *Available in different languages *Allows for an online library (3d Warehouse) for which users can contribute models

		*Supports third party plug-in programs. And enable placements of its models within Google Earth *Reference:* *www.sketchup.com/products/sketcup-pro*
	ALLPLAN is a subsidiary of the Nemetschek Group in Munich. A software that can be used by architects, civil engineers, contractors and facility managers. It can also allow construction cost to be managed while designing with the help of planning and visualization tools of BIM software that supports 2D and 3D modeling and over 50 file formats for example,	*Traceable design histories *Programmable Interface *Detailed Building Model *Data Exchange *Analyzing Model Data *Tracking Project Participants *Easy-to-use Task Management and so on. *Reference:* *www.allplan.com*
	Founded in 1985. Vectorworks contains	**Vectorworks Architect Features:**

|  | different categories of software's which include Vectorworks Designer, Architect, Landmark, Spotlight, Fundamentals, and Renderworks. It can be used by those in architecture, landscape, mechanical engineering, entertainment industries, etc. | *Seamless Interoperability:* support the exchange of concept models from Rhino or SketchUp, support the import and export of 3DM, SKP, and COLLADA file formats, as well as OBJ, STL, and 3DS, also offers for the creation and analysis of construction documents.
Multiuser Environment: Project sharing enables architects, interior designers, and others to unify their workflows by allowing the project team to work on the same Vectorworks file concurrently.
Superior Documentation: offers a broader array of drafting and annotation tools than other BIM applications.
*A quality BIM tool

Reference:
www.vectorworks.net/architect |
| | Developed by Bentley systems and was first released in the 1980s. It is an advanced architectural design | *Work collaboratively on designs
* Work in a personalized environment (that is, streamline your workflow and integrate with enterprise systems using a wide |

|
MicroStation® | production software and information modeling environment that enable users to create innovative designs for architecture, construction or engineering of any infrastructure including homes, roads, bridges, plants, skyscrapers and more. It also enables the performance simulation of architecture designs. MicroStation enables intrinsic Geo-coordination, hyper modeling, etc. | range of available tools to customize the user interface including Microsoft (VBA), .NET, C++, C# and user-defined macrons) *Visualize and analyze designs (for example perform analysis of real-world solar exposure and shading, apply real-time display styles to visualize models based on each object`s height, slope, aspect angle, and other embedded properties) *Produce animations and renderings *Layout and annotate drawings *Enforce standards (ensure proper application of organizational and project-specific standards and content, once designs are complete, use automated tools to check drawings for standards compliance) *Design with 3D parametric modeling Design in context (clearly understand existing conditions and accelerate design modeling workflows with the ability to easily |

		integrate imagery, point clouds, and 3D reality meshes into design and construction models)
		Reference: *www.bentley.com/en/products/product-line/modeling-and-visualization-software/microstation*
smartdraw	A diagramming software, that makes it easy to create home building and renovation plans quickly and easily. It can also be used to make flowcharts, organization charts project charts and so on.	*Quite easy for beginners (whether architects or not) to start with and advanced enough for professionals to create complex designs *Any SmartDraw drawing can be inserted into Word®, Excel ® and PowerPoint® and works fine on Dropbox®, Google Drive™, and One Drive ® *Runs on a Windows desktop, on a mac and online. *You can get quick support through call or email if you encounter any challenge from SmartDraw experts *Reference:* *www.smartdraw.com*
	DataCAD designed by professional architects	Its features include automatic door or window insertion, automated 3D

	and software engineers since 1984 is a professional-level AEC CAD program for architectural design, photo-realistic rendering, animation, and construction document creation and comes packaged with tools to simplify design and drafting.	framing and modeling, associative dimension and hatching, automated 3D framing and Teigha-based DXF/DWG translators. Enables the control of lighting, cast shadows, and apply texture maps to create compelling, 24-bit colour images of the latest design. *Reference: www.datacad.com*
	ProArchitect is an easy to use Building Information Modelling (BIM) software built for architects and novice users to help them design powerful 3D designs and visualizations for all types of construction and remodeling projects.	*ProArchitect supports file formats of other design packages for project sharing, they include SketchUp, 3DS, VRM and AutoCAD *Enable the extraction of drawing information such as elevation, plans, sections and details directly from models. *Provides photorealistic renderings *Creates complex roof geometry with ease *Comprehensive site and landscape design

		Reference: *www.cadsoft.com/products/pro-architect/*
floor planner	Founded in 2007, it is a design software that allows the designer to generate interactive floor plans and share them online (for personal or marketing p), helps with step by step guidance and handling.	*Equipped with an intuitive editor that allows for floor plans to be drawn in minutes *Enables for the design of interiors and exporting high-resolution images *Designs can be exported to PDF *iPad and iPhone application *Reference:* *www.floorplanner.com*
punch! SOFTWARE	A design software founded in 1998 by Navarre Digital Services Inc. it is a home and landscape design software	*Enables a designer to build a project from professionally designed floor plan, add details with the full-featured toolbox and an extensive library of named brand product, materials, and furnishings to generate unlimited home design ideas and floorplans *The perfect tool to design or enhance landscape projects and outdoor living spaces (features include comprehensive plant library, drag-and-drop designing, premade templates)

		*Enable interior designers to import or create a custom floorplan and pick from over 4000 3D objects to enhance interior design.
		*Advanced photo rendering
		*iPhone and iPad Apps
		*Finding and avoiding conflicts
		*Modulating materials and energy
		Reference:
		www.punchsoftware.com

Table 2: List of Some Architectural Design Software

(N: B Bearing in mind subsequent versions will show improved features of each software)

Using CAD comes with a price and requirements which proprietors refer to as system requirements. We may have the 'challenge' of voluminous pages to deal with if we are to review the system requirements for each of the software listed above. However, we will consider some basic requirements (or standards) that cut across many software. They include the following:

- **Random Access Memory (RAM) Memory:** This is the short-term memory of the machine and dictates how large a program or how many programs can be held in memory at once while the processor swallows away. The RAM is crucial for the overall machine performance. Minimum of 6GB RAM may not be bad and a max of 16GM + Ram will be superb indeed.

- **Storage Disk:** This is the memory of the PC for the storage of files; this is very vital as no data can make it to the RAM and processor cores unless it is first read from the hard disk drive. It influences the speed of the PC hence, the bigger the better.

- **Monitors:** The better the resolution, the better the designer gets a feel of his designs; thus, it is advisable to work with a screen with high resolution. 17" Monitor (1280 x 1024) is suitable but 17" Hi-Def Monitor (1920 x 1200) or 19"-24" Hi-Def Monitor, if it's a desktop, gives a better experience

- **Graphics Card:** This is a vital part of the machine which takes care of all the visual calculations of what can be seen on screen, especially when working in a 3D environment. It is equally important to look for a high-performance card put by Nvidia, Radeon or AMD ForePro series graphics card.

- **Graphics Processor:** This is often called the 'brains' of the computer and like the brain, it helps to do all the calculations and code-crunching which makes computer programs run. Speed (measured in megahertz and gigahertz) and a number of parallel processes determine the efficiency and effectiveness it needs. The right choice of processor is pertinent to CAD software's usually the minimum CAD PC requirements will be intel i5 processor or AMD Quad a better requirement will be the Intel Xenon Processor

- **Operating System (OS)**: This holds all the information and instructions the computer needs to be able to function properly. Windows 10 64-bit OS or newer is advisable considering how large some software programs can be.

The Printer: Another thing to consider in the use of CAD is that the drawing that has been produced in the computer system has to be printed by the use of a machine which will take the date and generate an output in the form of graphics or text on a surface (Paper) A printer. There are different types of printers classified as either impact or non-impact printers. Here are a few common printers used:

- **Inkjet and Deskjet** are two of the most commonly used printers today. Inkjet printers are non-impact printers, with its characteristics of less noise and essential in creating digital images on paper with the use of droplets of varying sizes. They make use of cartridges for printing in several colours.

- **Laser printers:** They make use of dry powdered ink and a laser beam for producing a fine dot matrix pater. They can be very useful for large productions of drawings.

- **Plotters or wide format printers;** These are large scale printers and known for their efficiency and effectiveness in producing line drawings.

Others include thermal printers, LCD and LED printers, line printers and so on.

Photocopier: A photocopier is also essential to make copies of drawings quickly and cheaply either in a coloured or black and white form.

Chapter Two

BASIC ELEMENTS, LAYOUTS AND PRESENTATIONS

2.0.   Lines and Drawing Units

Lines are very important in working drawings. Lines are used to communicating the thoughts, intents and purpose of the design. Every line used must have certain significance, significance that is conveyed through the line thickness and property. The understanding of the types of lines and it`s usage is paramount whether in manual or CAD. The basic common types of lines include:

- *Continuous thick Lines (Outline lines):*

Used for visible outlines (to enhance the main and important feature of the drawing), general details, existing buildings and landscaping in site plans. For example, in Figure 20, the thick line is not just used to enhance the closest feature, but clearly indicates and different the distance of objects.

- Continuous thin lines (Construction lines):

These are used for dimension leader lines, outline of adjacent parts, projection lines, intersection lines, hatching, headers and extension lines

- Hidden Lines: These are short dashed medium lines usually drawn approximately 2 millimeters apart. They show edges of objects not directly visible in the orthographic view or the building elements or objects.

Used to indicate objects that are part of the drawing that is not visible on the surface or objects hidden behind others.

- Continuous thin Zigzag lines: Long break lines that indicate when an object is not drawn in its entirety.

- Dashed Thin Lines with dots

— · — · — · — · — · — · — · — · — · — · —

Also referred to as the centre lines, used to indicate the centre of objects such as doors, walls, windows.

- Chain Lines (Centre Lines): Long dash lines with a short little dot, centre lines, locus line position of movable parts, parts situated in front of cutting plane and pirch circles.

Others include long thin dashed and double short dashed lines, long thin lines double dots,

The Various Use Of The Lines

- **To Communicate Depth**

Take for example the figure below, the use of the continuous thick and thin line to communicate depth and distance is exemplified, this should be evident in working drawings especially when drawing elevations and sections

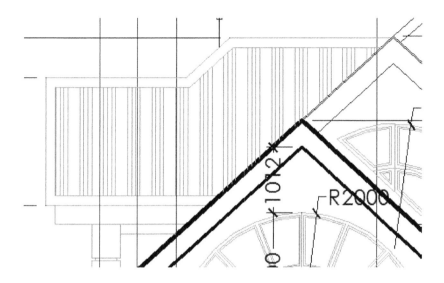

Figure 20: A partial elevation Drawing showing the line depth

When making use of lines to show objects, care must be taken to use lines to communicate depth and distance. Objects that seem to be far away can be shown with a faint line as seen in Figure 20.

- **Dimension Lines**

Dimension lines are lines drawn on and around a drawing, to show (by its calibration) the size of elements in a drawing. It is the measurement of any sort (linear and angular dimensions), usually scaled that shows the magnitude of various lines and elements. There are two types: 2 dimensional and 3 dimensional (length, width and height).

In a working drawing, all dimensions must be on one scale unless required otherwise. It is not necessary to indicate the measuring standard (like 600cm or 78m) since it will appear on the panel. Avoid the mixing of metrics and imperial units on the same drawing because it can be confusing. It is expedient that the architect or designer considers the following as it pertains to dimensions:

- Provide dimension lines that are clear, consistent in their format and accurate.
- Provide ample dimensions and verify that they are accurate.
- Dimensioning must be done externally and internally.
- The sums of parallel dimensions between the same points must be the same.
- Dimension lines should be faint (construction lines), while lettering should be bold (outline).
- Avoid conflict of dimension lines and drawing lines.
- Choose dimension lines that will capture so many parts of the drawings to be dimensioned.
- In dimensioning, cross lines are better than point lines.
- For every wall, there must be two or more-dimension lines reading the sizes of elements or spaces.

- Spaces that are too small (like a 225mm wall) can be dimensioned at an angle, (see fig. 21) directly on the top of the element.
- Angular and circular dimensions must be shown.

Dimension lines can come in any of these three styles:

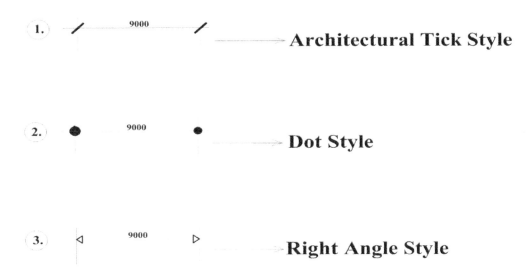

Figure 21a: Dimension styles

Note that the angle of the slant of the architectural thick is 45^0.

The common practice for architects when producing architectural working drawings is to use the architectural tick style dimension technique which is good for consistency.

Figure 21b: Dimension line terminologies

Figure 21c is a good example of how the extension line should relate with the object which is in direct contrast to the practice in figure 21d

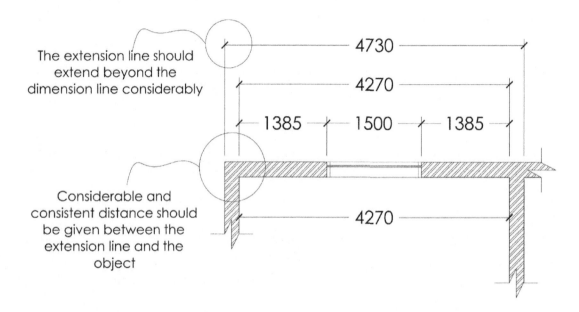

Figure 21c: Correct method of how extension lines should relate with objects

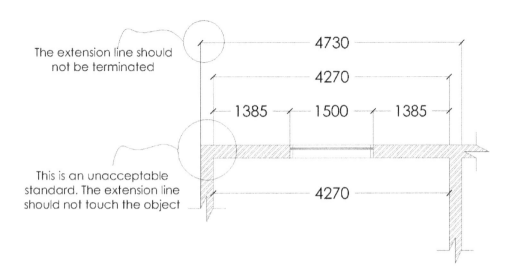

The extension line should not be terminated

4730

4270

1385 — 1500 — 1385

This is an unacceptable standard. The extension line should not touch the object

4270

Figure 21d: The wrong way of using the extension lines

Overall dimensions must be shown externally on the plan, elevation, and sections and must appear in bigger font size (see figure 21c and 21d) and the vertical, horizontal and diagonal dimensions must be shown.

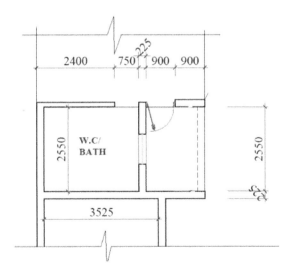

2400   750 900 900
225

W.C/
BATH

2550

2550

3525

Figure 21e: Showing horizontal and vertical dimension

Space names should be written straight (see fig. 21f and 21g) not minding whether the space is at an angle or not and the font-size of the text on the dimension line that sums up the size of figures on another dimension line is usually larger. Inclined dimensioning (see figure 21e) is allowed where the space cannot accommodate the figures

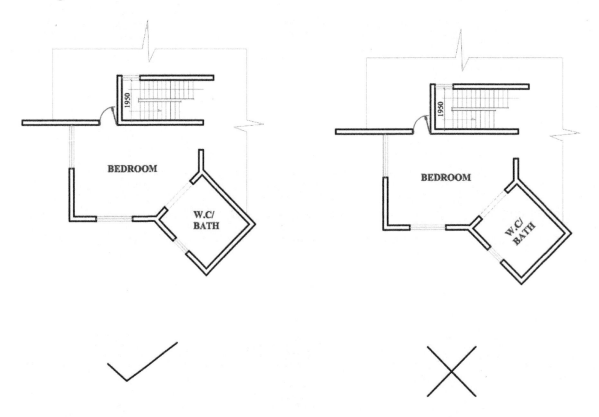

Figure 21f: Correct way of naming room spaces of naming room spaces

Figure 21g: Wrong-way

- **Drawing Units**

The unit of measurement across the globe is quite different from one region to another, for example in the United States, it is known as 'imperial units' (feet and inches), in some parts of Europe, they use the old European metric standard (centimetres (cm) and decimals of a centimetre), while other countries use the standard international unit based on metric system where all the dimensions are measured in mm. Nigeria, in particular, uses this. It is essential for every architect or designer to understand the conversion rate for each of the units and be familiar with them.

It may be an old practice, but the dimensioning of a floor plan or any other detail drawing may be drawn to reflect an alternative unit as shown in figure 22 this may be particularly necessary for setting out to help other allied professions who may have been used to other drawing units.

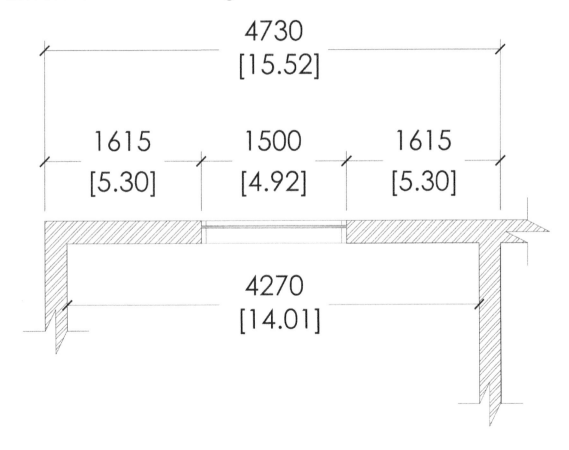

Fig. 22 Showing dimension showing alternative units (on top is in mm and below in feet)

Though this method sure may consume much space, it is preferable to round it up to one decimal place to avoid any form of clumsiness that may be seen on the sheet, but it sure reduces the effort of calculating on-site during setting out.

Section Line

Conventional signs for section lines (broken lines) should be used, and the line should be seen to pass through all the elements and spaces intended to be shown. It is wrong to stop a section line and continue it at another end. Section lines are usually cut through interesting areas or spaces that may require some clarity. All elements appearing in elevation on the axis of the section must be shown faintly in the sectional drawing. The direction of section lines can be altered to show an important feature in the design, see figure 23b. However, it is very imperative to note that a change in section line position is linked with a continuous thin line as seen in Figure23b. All section lines must be numbered or named.

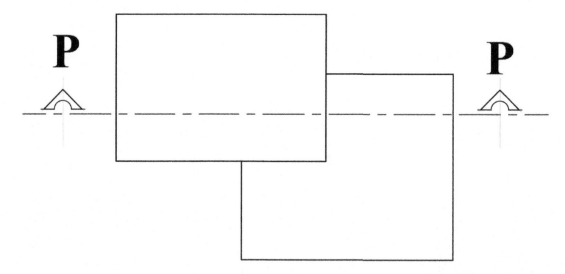

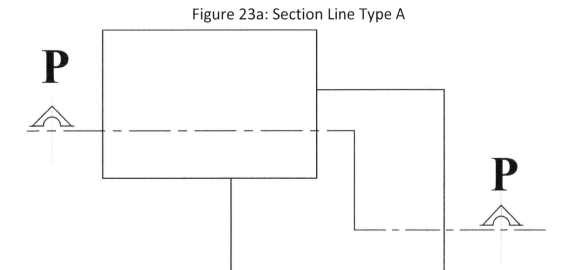

Figure 23a: Section Line Type A

Figure 23b: Section Line Type B *(notice that the link is established by a continuous thin line)*

All section lines and detailed drawings must be labeled, numbered or named for easy identification and reference.

2.1. Lettering

Lettering is the creation of text, dimensions and notes to apply to an object or surface through the use of manual or digital means. The text is of paramount importance in working drawings and should be clearly differentiated from those used in presentation drawings. Written communications are necessary to convey the concepts of the designer to the client, contractor, and other allied professionals.

Wherever the text is existing for example in gridlines, dimensions, plans, drawing title blocks, specifications, schedules, etc., it should be clear and legible enough so that it can be read and understood by a worker on-site. What is the point of making the lettering complicated and difficult for it to be read and understood for the purpose of constructions? Simplicity should not be misunderstood to depict a lack of creativity or the absence of beauty. Often times, it is needed so as to carry others along and communicate with everyone else.

Basic requirements cutting across the text style must be taken into consideration, this includes the **font, size, height** and **standard effects.**

The font

The font style should be consistent, legible and maintain some degree of clarity in expression. It is necessary that the designer avoid very complicated text like the one seen below and its likes.

A B C D E F G H I J K L M N O P Q R S T U V W X Y Z

A B C D E F G H I J K L M N O P Q R S T U V W X Y Z

A B C D E F G H I J K L M N O P Q R S T U V W X Y Z

They indeed look captivating but can pose a great danger in interpreting[10] (oops!) the drawings and its specifications,

Below are common fonts used in production drawings:

FONT	SAMPLE
Times New Roman	A B C D E F G H I J K L M N O P Q R S T U V W X Y Z a b c d e f g h i j k l m n o p q r s t u v w x y z

---

[10] The intricacy in this text may take twice as much time to read, understand and interpret the drawing and can be frustrating... They indeed look captivating but can pose a great danger in interpreting

	1 2 3 4 5 6 7 8 9 0
Arial	A B C D E F G H I J K L M N O P Q R S T U V W X Y Z a b c d e f g h i j k l m n o p q r s t u v w x y z 1 2 3 4 5 6 7 8 9 0
Simplex	A B C D E F G H I J K L M N O P Q R S T U V W X Y Z a b c d e f g h i j k l m n o p q r s t u v w x y z 1 2 3 4 5 6 7 8 9 0
lucida console	A B C D E F G H I J K L M N O P Q R S T U V W X Y Z a b c d e f g h i j k l m n o p q r s t u v w x y z 1 2 3 4 5 6 7 8 9 0
Century Gothic	A B C D E F G H I J K L M N O P Q R S T U V W X Y Z a b c d e f g h i j k l m n o p q r s t u v w x y z 1 2 3 4 5 6 7 8 9 0
RomanC	A B C D E F G H I J K L M N O P Q R S T U V W X Y Z a b c d e f g h i j k l m n o p q r s t u v w x y z 1 2 3 4 5 6 7 8 9 0
Calibri	A B C D E F G H I J K L M N O P Q R S T U V W X Y Z a b c d e f g h i j k l m n o p q r s t u v w x y z 1 2 3 4 5 6 7 8 9 0
Tahoma	A B C D E F G H I J K L M N O P Q R S T U V W X Y Z a b c d e f g h i j k l m n o p q r s t u v w x y z 1 2 3 4 5 6 7 8 9 0

Table 3: Lettering Styles and sample

Though sometimes, it's the practice of some architects to combine fonts, some prefer to use a particular kind of font for notes, drawing titles, and another dimension.

Font size and Height

The font style size can be produced to either be bold, bold italic, italic or regular (this can be done manually or digitally) but care must be taken to maintain consistency throughout. The best manual method could be the use of stencils or for thin lines to be used as a guide for any type of fonts. In the use of manual methods, the text height could be 2.5mm, 3.0mm or 3.5mm in max, depending on the scale of the drawing for notes, names of room spaces, dimensions et cetera), 5mm for drawing titles, axis numbering).

In the use of a digital method (CAD), it simplifies the whole process. For example with AutoCAD, you can set the correct height for the plot scales or use AutoCAD annotative scaling for that purpose.

Standards effects

The spacing between letters, numbers and characters[11] should be adequate (not too wide, too narrow, too close or too loose)

---

[11] Width factor

2.2. Symbols and Notations

The are several working drawing symbols and notations which cut across, conventions for doors and windows, construction elements, finishing's, materials et cetera.

In working drawing, the architect must not give the reader of the drawing any room for assumptions or doubts. This means that he has to be thorough in his drafting. In preparing this document (architectural working drawing), the architect must try to adhere to conventional design rules, symbols and standards, which are not strict in the sense of scientific modules, but when not adhered to, might tell a different story, and may be interpreted wrongly by the builder. As much as there are conventional ways of producing drawings, the reality is that many options are available to the architect in achieving the same aim.

These rules are:

- Conventional design signs must be used as shown in some of the architecture graphical symbols in Figure 24 below.

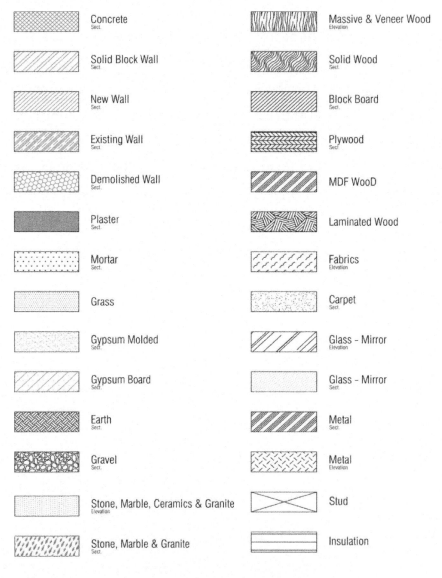

Figure 24: Material Hatches

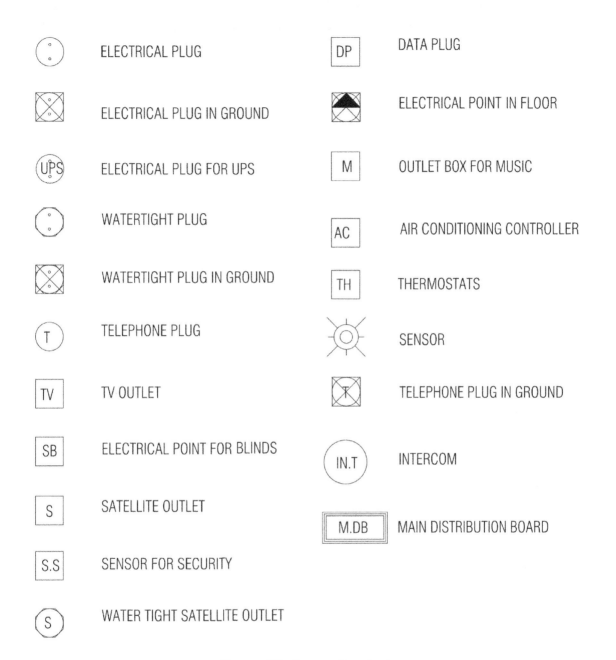

ELECTRICAL PLUG	DATA PLUG
ELECTRICAL PLUG IN GROUND	ELECTRICAL POINT IN FLOOR
ELECTRICAL PLUG FOR UPS	OUTLET BOX FOR MUSIC
WATERTIGHT PLUG	AIR CONDITIONING CONTROLLER
WATERTIGHT PLUG IN GROUND	THERMOSTATS
TELEPHONE PLUG	SENSOR
TV OUTLET	TELEPHONE PLUG IN GROUND
ELECTRICAL POINT FOR BLINDS	INTERCOM
SATELLITE OUTLET	MAIN DISTRIBUTION BOARD
SENSOR FOR SECURITY	
WATER TIGHT SATELLITE OUTLET	

Figure 25: Power Symbols

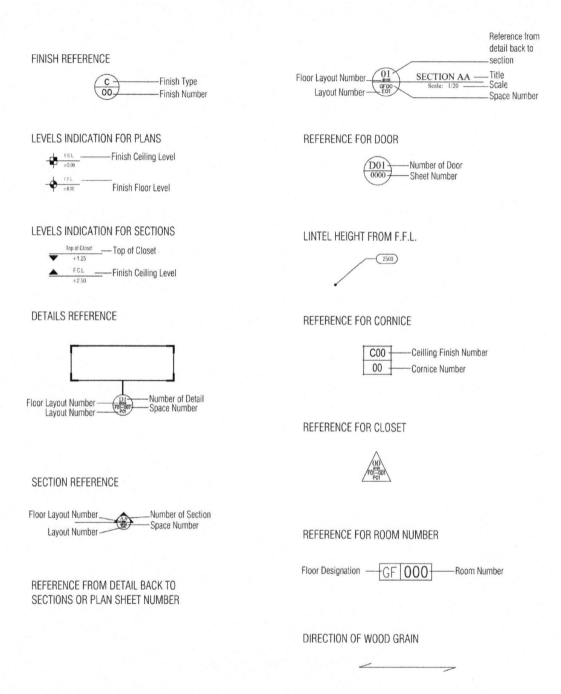

Figure 26: Drafting Symbols

FINISH LEGEND

CA	Carpet
CT	Ceramic Tiles
FA	Fabrics
GL	Glazing
GR	Granite
GY	Gypsum Material
MA	Marble
MR	Mirror
MW	Metal Work
PL	Plastic Laminate
PT	Paint
QZ	Quartz
ST	Stone
SF	Special Finish
WM	Wall Covering Material
WD	Wood Finish

Figure 27: Finish Symbols

Figure 28: HVAC Symbols

2.3. Referencing

This is used in a working drawing to identify special details that may require further clarity or explanation. For example, man as a tripartite personality comprises the spirit, soul and body. All three have different functions but should not be separated from each other, the spirit is not meant to exist alone on earth, neither the soul or the body. The man cannot be said to be complete without one or the other. The working drawing is part of a tripartite relationship. It does not exist alone; it is a constituent of a concept called the '**complete information package'**. This concept consists of the working drawings, bill of quantities and specifications. They don`t exist without the other, together they form the complete building package needed for any project.

It is the responsibility of the architect to **structure** the drawings in such a professional way that it contains fundamental and vital information needed for other allied professionals to work with, and for the production of the bill of quantities (to compute) and specifications (to amplify).

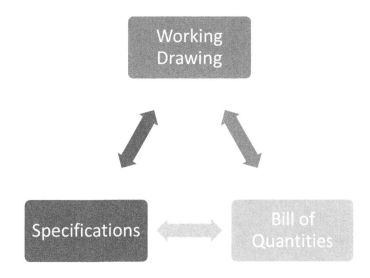

Figure 25: The structure of a Complete Information Package

Care must be taken to provide necessary information on each sheet that will help other allied professions, hence the title 'referencing' for this section. The whole idea of the 'referencing' considers basic ways an architect can structure (using, codes, standard symbols and notations) the drawing so that in a bid to communicate, so that the architect does not end up mystifying and complicating the production drawings. Proper reference minimizes unnecessary clusters we find in the location plans and prepared on a separate sheet or as a compendium of another document.

Drawing title

Often times some designers when producing working drawings will just resort to name the drawing whichever way pleases them, as long as it captures the title at the bottom, this should not be the conventional method though; For example in Figure 29a, the designer had quite a nice font style which may be good for presentation drawings but not a standard way of representing the drawing title for every sheet.

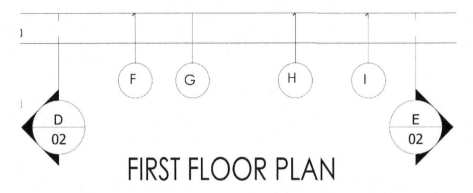

Figure 29a: Wrong representation for drawing title

The drawing title must contain certain basic information which gives breath to referencing that cuts across details, door and window tags, etc. It should contain the drawing name, the view number (sheet number) and the scale for the particular drawing as seen below.

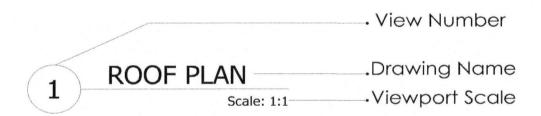

Figure 29b: Standard representation for drawing titles

In very complex drawings, the sheet number may take different codes, for example, first-floor drawings contain multiple sheets, thus the sheet number may be coded by the architect to be 1A01. Let's assume, '1' represents level one, 'A' is tagged area A and '01' the number of that particular sheet.

Section Symbol

It is not sufficient to just have a section line cutting through an object or a drawing, there are certain information that must be shown on the section symbol as seen below. The section number can be any code by the architect, it could be any alphabet (A-Z) but not necessarily numbers (to avoid clashes or confusion with the sheet number) except in complex projects where the architect may still use codes like A^1, B^1, C^1 etc. The sheet number represents the particular sheet the section appears in.

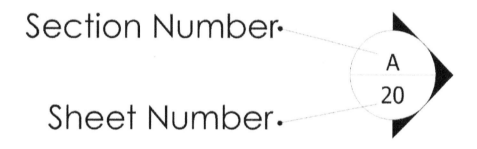

Figure 30: Section Symbol

Numbering Spaces

In complex projects where the spaces are numerous e.g. in a two-hundred-bedroom hotel, the designer may resort to numbering the spaces, from the entrance lobby to all the internal spaces, in a logical order, to assist in detailing, scheduling, and specification. The numbering is usually circled at the center of the space. The numbering should follow a sequence according to the floor levels e.g., basement—B01, B02, B03... Ground floor—101,102,103.... Second floor---

201,202,203. It helps in bidding and project construction. If a drawing refers to information found elsewhere in the drawing, it must be thoroughly cross-referenced. However, this does work for simple projects too, the rooms could be numbered (see the figure below).

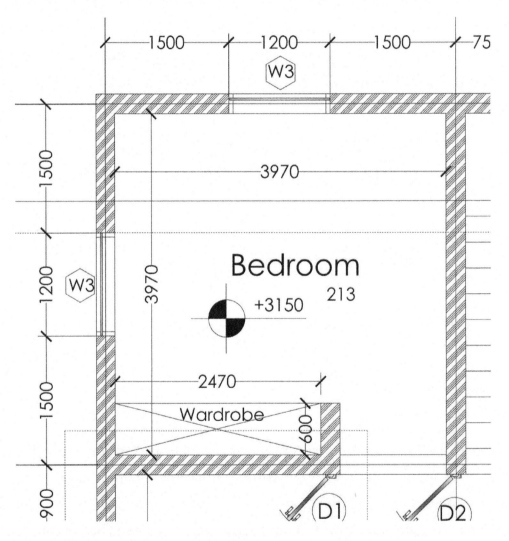

Figure 31a: Partial Plan (showing a bedroom numbered)

The bedroom was numbered '016' this number could help in preparing the finish for the particular space. However, some architects resort to a direct way of reference which will be necessary for finishing schedule, 'especially' for small projects, see the example below

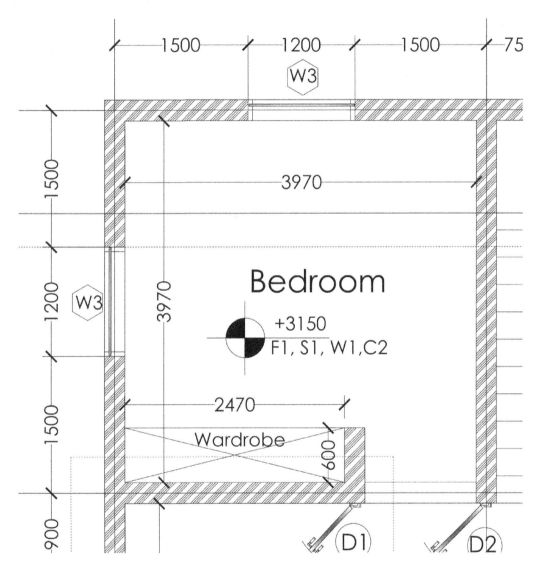

Figure 31b: Showing another purpose for room tags

In this example above, the architect resorted to using the code F1, S1, W1, C2 where F1 represents floor finish, so there could be F2 in another room space. The S1 represents skirting, while the W1 represents the wall finish, and C2 the ceiling finish. The code for the finish itself may be better understood in a separate sheet called 'finish schedule'.

Window and Door Tags

The common mistake that is observable in most working drawings is for the symbol for the window and door to be the same, but that is an unprofessional practice. Here is a good example for each window tag.

Figure 32a: Window and Door Tags

Care should be taken to notice the different shapes of the tags. The figure below gives an example of how to show the tag on the location plan (floorplan, elevation or sections). These tags are further used to prepare door and window schedule which we may see in the other discourse.

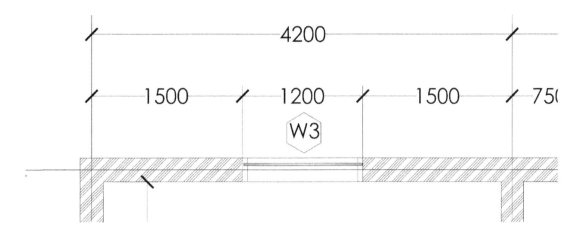

Figure 32b: Proper Position for window Tags

Call Out Tags

In working drawings, major and minor details should be shown to understand the constituent parts of the building. To do so, it is necessary to 'call-out' that particular details from the location plan and explains *'why you called it out'.* That is quite funny we guess, but it is the truth and if the architect-in-training does not understand the reason behind his actions and how to make it clear to others it will be devastating. No wonder many students and architects-in-training struggle with details because the 'why' and 'how' has not been understood. However, if one understands the 'why' and 'how' of every call-out much ambiguity will be minimized. The call-out tags are represented to standard. Below is an example to show the detail reference symbol.

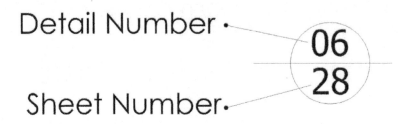

Figure 33: Detail reference Symbol

2.4. Gridlines

The term connotes different meaning in several professions, for example in MS[12] word it is a column separator, or row separator, in geography, it is a series of numbered horizontal and perpendicular lines that divide a map into squares to form a grid, a process that enables any point to be located by a system of rectangular coordinates. Though they share some similarities in their usage they are different.

In working drawings, gridlines provide the framework for the design of any two or three-dimensional surface. It helps to create order and reduce chaos. Gridlines are the most powerful tools that help architects to present their works in a professional manner.

Gridlines offer structure and aid in the organization of data, allowing the reader to easily locate and comprehend information on the drawing. It assists individuals with little experience in graphic communication to articulate lines, in proper alignment of elements, proper positioning of structural systems and general composition of the design. It adds scale to the drawing and aids in the effective articulation of the various spaces.

---

[12] Microsoft

Components of the drawing are articulated using block (usually calculated per square meter) system location. Gridlines can be symmetrically or asymmetrically placed, depending on the structural system and elements. The horizontal and vertical lines are named differently, e.g. **horizontal** = A, B C, D[13]... **vertical** = 1, 2, 3, 4. It is normally used in complex designs where juxtaposed lines could create visual conflict. Sometimes, radial grids are used in circular or curved structures for the same purpose.

Drawings drawn with grid lines can be particularly useful, in the sense that dimensions can be taken directly if need be (when there is minor unclarity) for the purpose of setting out on the site.

Figures 33a and 33b shows drawing done in grid lines. Figure 33a letters are wrongly placed while Figure 33b is correctly done.

---

[13] When the alphabets exceed 26, letters like A', B'/AA/BB/AA', BB'

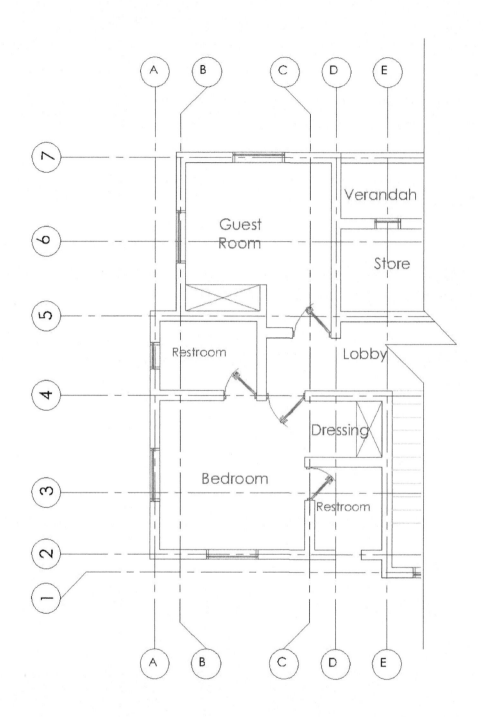

Figure 33a: Wrongly placed grid figures

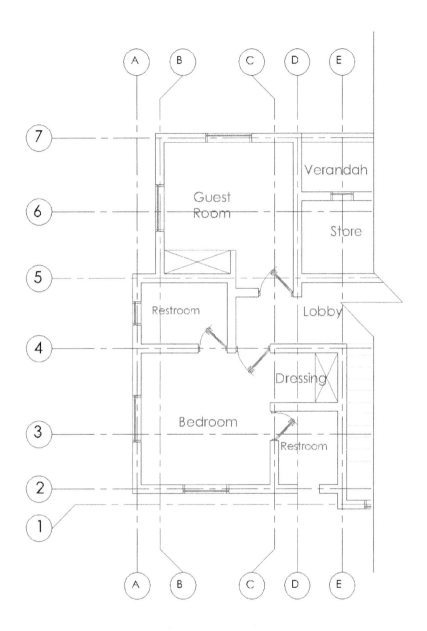

Figure 33b: Rightly placed grid figures

99

2.5. Drawing Panels

The title block is very important because it makes the drawing to be 'admitted' in cases of arbitration or during litigation. The drawing may require a check and approval by a registered architect to ensure that the designer conforms to all the requirements. The panel can be placed at the bottom (horizontal panel) of the paper as shown below in figure 32a or can also be placed at the right-hand side (vertical panel) of the paper as shown in figure 32b. The content of the panel will include a section for notes. The information on the note will include, but not limited to the dimension standard used and the foundation depth determinant, instructions from the Architect to the builders and any other vital information that was not captured in the working drawing but required for the smooth running of the project.

The drawing must be titled. The panel and body must provide all necessary information including the following:

- the proposed project name and address,
- the client`s name,
- the architects' firm name, address and details (including logo),
- the drawing title,
- the drawing date,
- the sheet number and size,
- the project and drawing number
- drawing scale
- project status (planning approval)
- Project team details
- Revision bar
- Drawing notes and so on

The panel may be horizontal or vertical, depending on the specified requirement. In most cases especially in practice, firms have a standard for their panels, changing only a little information from one project to another.

2.5. Perspective Drawings

There are several books on perspective drawings like the perspective drawing handbook by Joseph D`Amelio that will give any student of architecture a good grasp on perspective drawings. But it is tangential to working drawings, because it also sets the tone for reality, the relationship of objects to one another, only that this time it is more spatial. As a student you will find perspective to be important in the use of lines to communicate depth or distances. "Perspective" properly refers to any of various graphic techniques for depicting volumes and spatial relationships on a flat surface, such as size perspective and atmospheric perspective (Ching, 2011). In perspective drawing there are basic concepts to bear in mind, they include

The **horizon** is the visible, definite line or point for which the sky meets the land or water below. Generally speaking, this line affects the placement of the vanishing point(s) as well as the scene`s eye level.

The **orthogonal lines** are lines which are directed to a vanishing point in a perspective drawing.

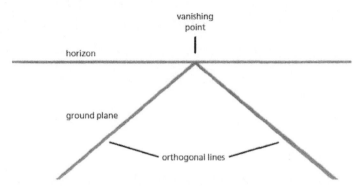

Figure 33c: Sample description of Perspective terms

The **Vanishing point** is the point at which parallel lines appear to converge in the distance.

The **Ground Plane is** the horizontal surface below the horizon which could be land or water.

The **vantage point** is different from the vanishing point, it is the place from which a scene is viewed. Some factors affect the vantage point, they include the placement of the horizon and the vanishing points.

There three types of perspectives, they include the following:

- One-Point Perspective: Linear perspective that has just one vanishing point
- Two Point Perspective: Linear perspective that makes use of two vanishing points placed at the far left and right in most cases.
- Multi-Point (three-point) Perspective: This is type of perspective drawing with more than two vanishing points, Although this depends on the complexity of the scene.

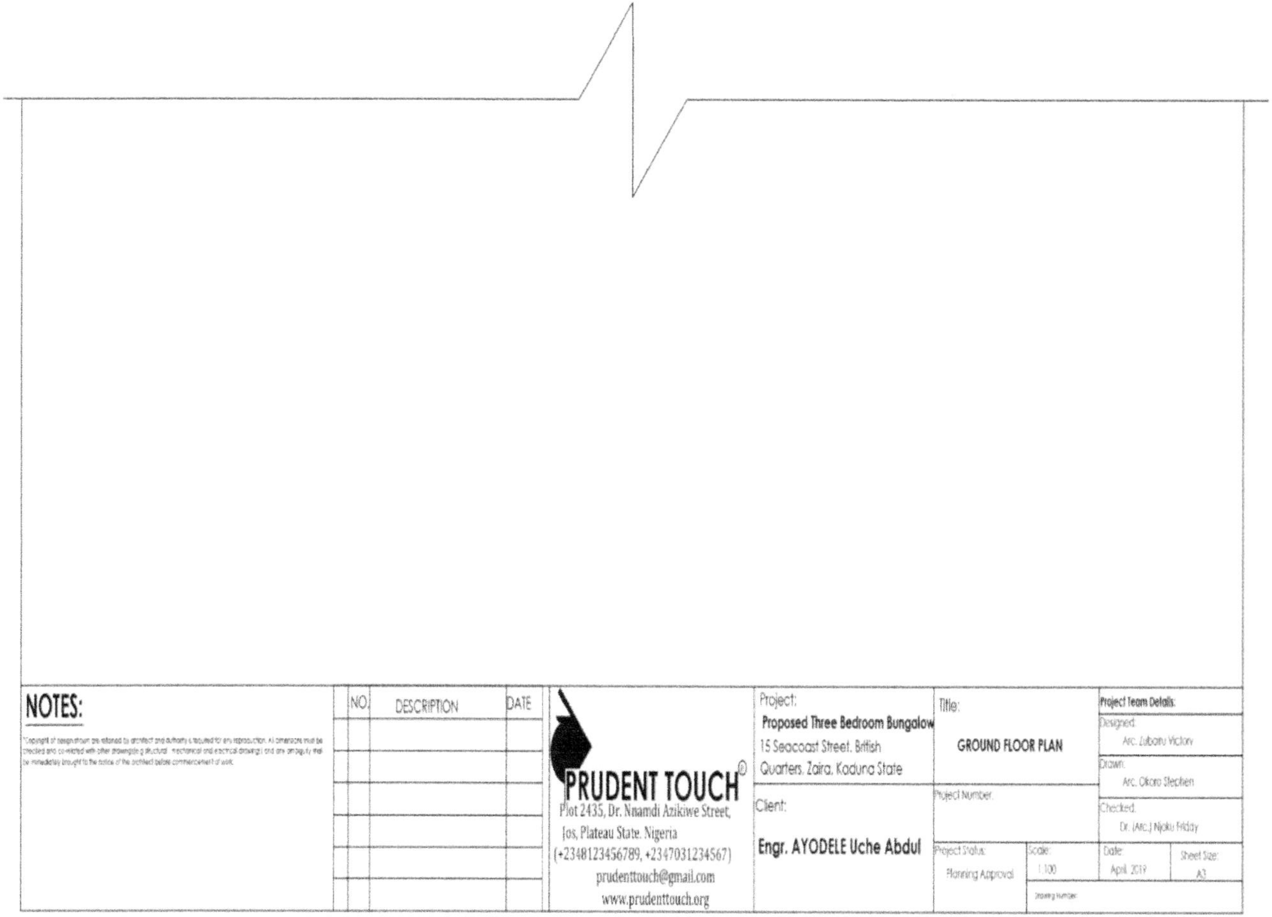

NO	DESCRIPTION	DATE

PRUDENT TOUCH®
Plot 2435, Dr. Nnamdi Azikiwe Street,
Jos, Plateau State, Nigeria
(+2348123456789, +2347031234567)
prudenttouch@gmail.com
www.prudenttouch.org

Project:
Proposed Three Bedroom Bungalow
15 Seacoast Street, British
Quarters, Zaria, Kaduna State

Client:
Engr. AYODELE Uche Abdul

Title:
GROUND FLOOR PLAN

Project Number:

Project Status		Scale: 1:100
Planning Approval		Drawing Number

Project Team Details:
Designed: Arc. Lubomi Victory
Drawn: Arc. Okoro Blessen
Checked: Dr (ARC) Njoku Friday

Date: April 2019	Sheet Size: A3

Figure 34a: Horizontal Drawing Panel

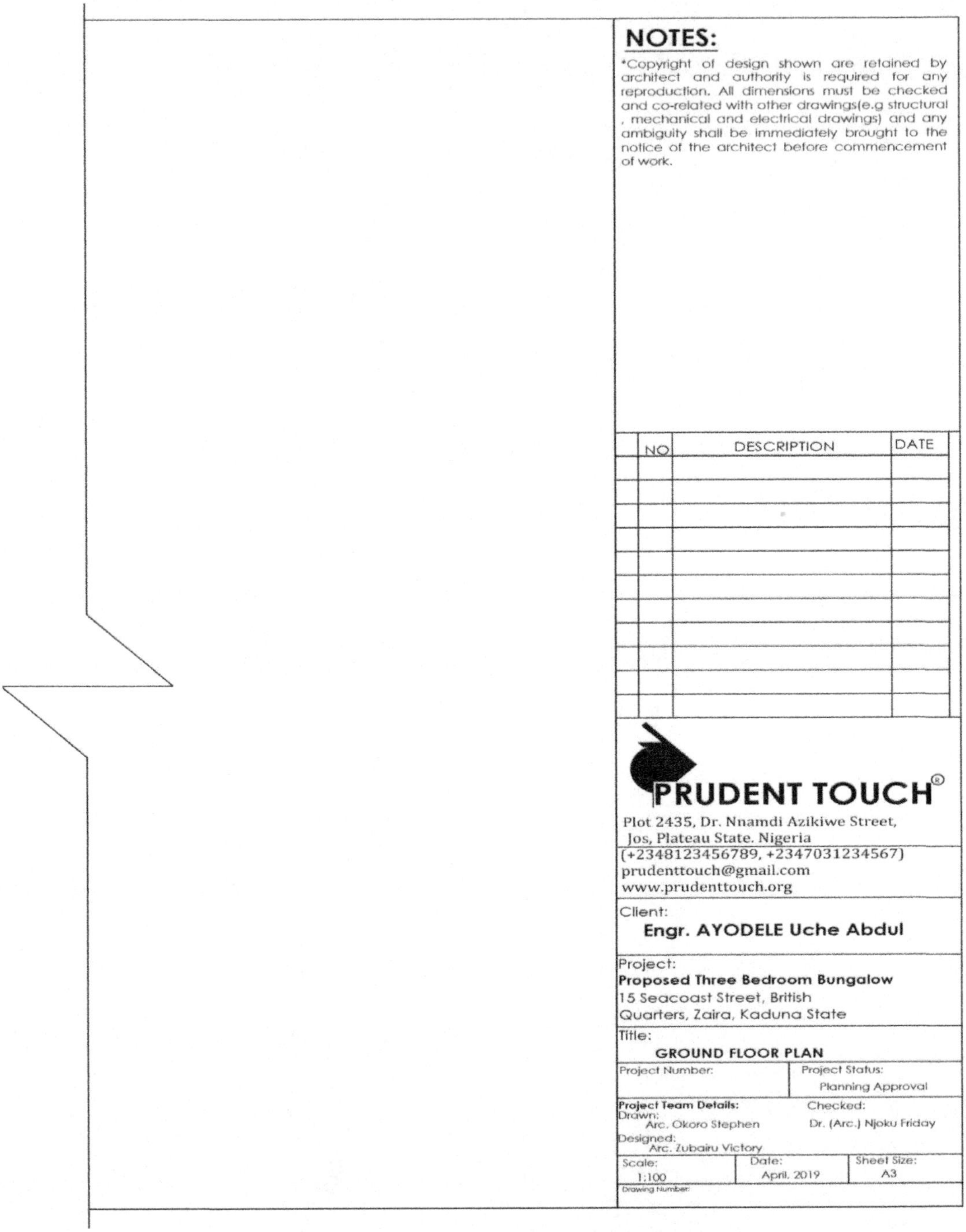
NOTES:
*Copyright of design shown are retained by architect and authority is required for any reproduction. All dimensions must be checked and co-related with other drawings(e.g structural , mechanical and electrical drawings) and any ambiguity shall be immediately brought to the notice of the architect before commencement of work.
NO
DESCRIPTION
DATE
PRUDENT TOUCH®
Plot 2435, Dr. Nnamdi Azikiwe Street, Jos, Plateau State. Nigeria
(+2348123456789, +2347031234567)
prudenttouch@gmail.com
www.prudenttouch.org
Client:
Engr. AYODELE Uche Abdul
Project:
Proposed Three Bedroom Bungalow
15 Seacoast Street, British Quarters, Zaira, Kaduna State
Title:
GROUND FLOOR PLAN
Project Number:
Project Status:
Planning Approval
Project Team Details:
Drawn:
Arc. Okoro Stephen
Checked:
Dr. (Arc.) Njoku Friday
Designed:
Arc. Zubairu Victory
Scale:
1:100
Date:
April, 2019
Sheet Size:
A3
Drawing Number:

Figure 34b: Vertical Drawing Panel

The architect may be required to present and or submit working drawings in hard and soft copies for other consultants, or for bidding as the case may be. The format for presentation leaves an indelible impression on the users. As such, packaging is very important. The neatness and organization of the working drawing convey a conviction that the architect is competent and knows his onions. The variety of projects makes it impossible to have fixed rules as to how to draw the panels and arrange the drawings, but one of the qualities of a good architect is to know how to organize drawings in a sheet for optimum clarity and aesthetics. The size and type of sheet depend on the requirements of the local authority or the designer. It is not good for a sheet to be too busy or overcrowded, neither should it be too scanty. Balancing of work on sheets should be practiced and perfected in order to have a good drawing. All drawing sheets must have a panel containing information about the drawing and its owners. The panel must be consistent with all the drawings required for that project.

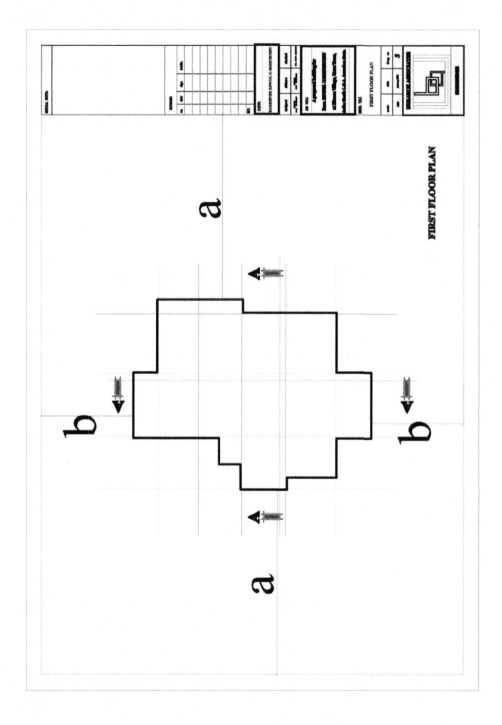

Figure 35a: A typical drawing sheet showing a sketch plan

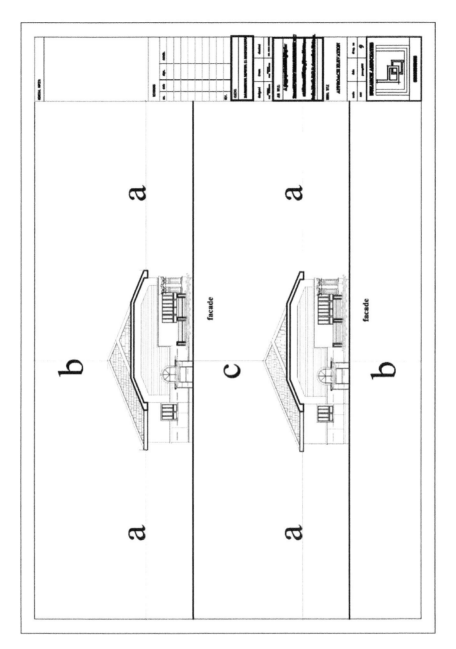

Figure 35b: A Typical Drawing sheet showing sketch Elevations (quite okay for smaller projects)

The drawing must be properly dimensioned and every element on the drawing should have at least two spots where its dimension can be read from.

- All spaces in the drawings must be named irrespective of their size.

- There must be a structural pattern usually in a grid format, whether symmetric or asymmetric and should be used to arrange the spaces.

- Prioritization of lines becomes very imperative if we want to avoid conflicting lines. Follow an order of importance to allocate line weights, e.g. Wall-Space.name—Element—Dimension.line—Dimensioned.figures—Drawing.notes—Furniture--Finishing.

- Space names should be located as central as possible on the spaces in the drawing and should be bold enough. In fact, space names assume the second position in allocation of line weight.

- The emphasis paid to furnish in presentation drawing is played down on in a working drawing to reduce line conflicts. In every complex drawing, furnishings is entirely eschewed and can only surface when detailed drawings are done

- In very detailed working drawings, the roof pattern, beams, lintels including any important element(s) above the window seal will appear on the floor plan, usually in hidden lines.

- In working drawings, a 0 datum is normally assumed at the point of the ground level. All changes in levels on plan and elevation must be represented with a line and the heights of the changes are represented like this $^{+}150$, $^{-}150$, and $^{+}300$ as the case may be. The change in level can be negative if the change is below the ground level (G.L.) and positive if the change is above the ground level because the assumption is that our datum

(0) is on the ground level. Figure 4 shows the various changes in the level of the plan.

- All working drawings (Plan, elevation, sections) must-have drawing notes (specification write-up), usually written in a font-size less than half of the space-name font, and having a wave-like arrow pointing to the element.

Chapter Three

GENERAL ARRANGEMENT DRAWINGS

3.0. Site Plan

The site plan is usually the first drawing to be presented after the preliminary sheets unless the location site plan is required. In presentation drawing, it is a chopper view of all that will be on the site when completed, including trees undulations, natural and artificial elements and so on. The recommended scales for site plans are usually 1:500, 1:200, depending on the size of land and scale of work.

For a properly finished site plan, it must show:

- The position of the north arrow on all plans.
- Dimensions of the site from beacon to beacon.
- All structures on the site plan must be named properly.
- The bearing and beacon numbers must be indicated.
- The entrance to the building with an arrow.
- All features on-site to be retained (natural and man-made features) will appear in the drawing in their exact position.

- The existing roads; major and minor (including their names) and walkways on-site will appear on the working drawing.
- Adjoining structures, sites and properties, natural and artificial features, utilities (like high tension mast, drainage pipe or gutter) will appear on the drawing.
- The topography lines and size with respect to a known datum should be shown on the site plan.
- Show the ground floor level, ramp head and tail, stairs pavements, driveways in relation to a chosen datum.
- Indicate the invert levels of all drains and their discharge points.
- All the setbacks and building lines should be indicated.
- All utilities like public water supply, well or borehole, electric poles should be shown.
- Dimension points from the building to known positions or established reference points on the boundary should be indicated for easy setting out. It is advisable to choose positions that are parallel to the building because of ease in setting out.
- In the working drawing site plan, the roof is not necessary. One should ensure that the drawing is the exact shape of the structure from the window sill level. It is wrong to assume a shape because one may get a wrong reading when setting out.
- The space to be occupied by the structure may be hatched and labeled.
- The proper type and swing of the vehicular and pedestrian gate.
- The finishing material for all pedestrian walkways, roads, lawns, retaining walls, kerbs, etc., with rendering and specification writing.
- Indicate statutory development data which will include the following

- Area of the landmass.
- Area of the used area.
- Percentage of the area used on the site.

N:B: It is not necessary to show the depth of the building and other elements using shadow casting.

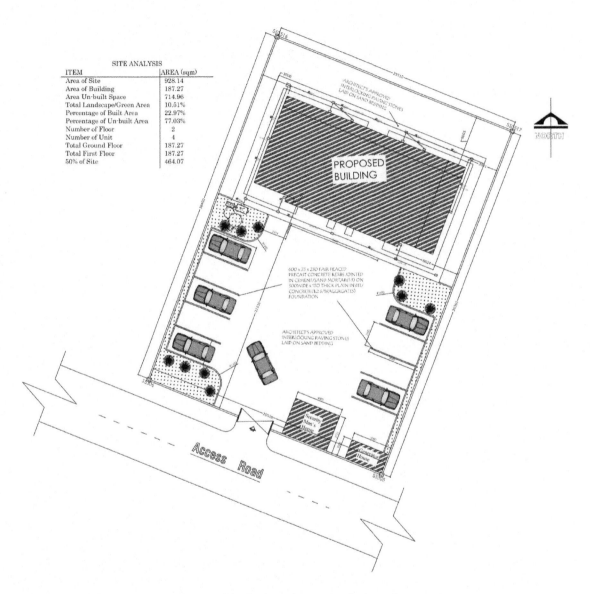

Figure 36: A simple typical site plan

114

3.1. Floor Plan

It is the top view horizontal section of a building cut through the house at an assumed height of about 1000mm – 1500mm above the floor. The general assumption is that a floor plan is cut horizontally slightly above the window sill level as if lifting off the top. The floor plan cuts further up where the windows and doors are. Thus, the walls show a sectional view of the type of block wall used.

The floor plan is the heart of any set of architectural drawings. The number of plans will depend on the number of floors the structure is going either above or below the ground level. Floor plans are the preliminary drawings that determine how the building will turn out eventually. A properly drawn plan reduces the confusion encountered in producing other drawings.

Often times the floor plan is repeated a number of times to show different categories of information, such as electrical plan, reflected ceiling plan, etc., thus the floor plan should contain fundamental and elemental information which forms the bases for other drawings. In each case, the floor plan is drawn to carry unique information peculiar to the type of plan Usually the recommended scales are 1:200, 1:100 and 1:50, as the case may be.

The following are the details the floor plan should contain:

- Dimensions: Overall dimensions of buildings on all sides must be indicated, Internal dimensions of all rooms, corridors, terraces, cantilevers, and various openings should be indicated, Internal dimensions of all recesses, wardrobes, cupboards and counters. Furthermore, the width of all doors, windows and other openings (arch, latches, etc.) should be indicated
- All the spaces should be named and numbered.
- Fitted furniture tags, sunscreen tags, etc.

115

- Callouts for layouts and assembly drawings
- Relevant services location
- Indicate the type of walls (brick, stone, timber or block wall) and type of floor finish for all spaces.
- All floor levels should be indicated including the stair risers.
- Indicate the hidden lines; all beams, overhangs, cantilevers and roof type.
- All door and window swings, slides or roller shutters must be indicated.
- Floor plans should have grid lines vertically and horizontally. One of the sides should be numbered while alphabets are used on the other side shown in figure 37.
- Doors and windows should be numbered according to their size and type.
- All installations and fixtures in the building should be labeled in their positions.
- When floors are typical, the number of floors should appear on the plan.
- All section lines properly numbered should show on the plan.
- The North point should be shown.
- Indicate the direction of flights at staircases and all level changes.
- Widths of all threads and staircases and all level changes.
- Indicate the entrance to the building using an arrow.

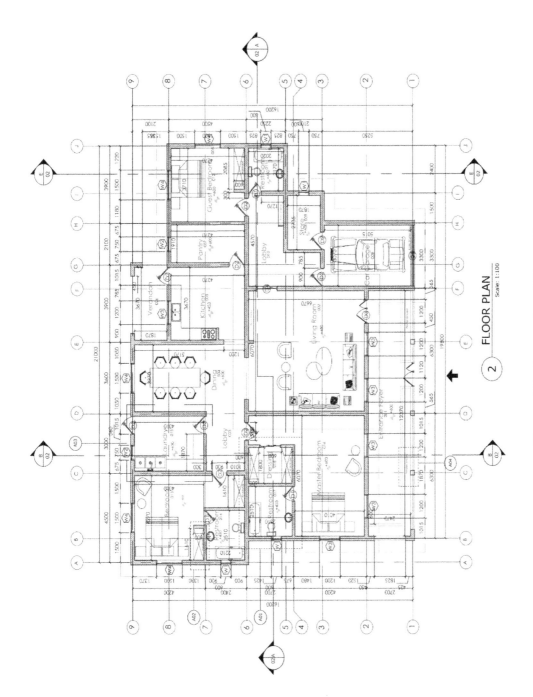

FLOOR PLAN
Scale: 1:100

Figure 37: A sample of Floor Plan

3.2. Reflected Ceiling Plan (RCP)

The reflected ceiling plan is part of the general arrangement drawing because it communicates the nature and locations of basic systems (lighting fixtures, smoke detectors, mechanical (HVAC) air diffusers, communication systems, and so on). It is drawn with the assumption that a designer from a particular point is looking downward at the floor through a clear glass ceiling or the other way round as if the floor were a mirror which shows the ceiling. What the designer sees by looking at the ceiling is what will be represented as the ceiling plan.

The ceiling plan should show lighting fixtures (luminaires; direct, indirect, direct-indirect, diffuse, etc.), sprinkler heads, HVAC devices and so on. The RCP should show all walls, partitions, and core elements as seen on the floor plan. The architect or interior designer can resort to using standard symbols to represent any fixture on the ceiling plan. The RCP should be drawn to scale (similar scale with the floor plan) and the symbols drawn to scale too. However, sometimes it not realistic as some fixtures like the miniature spotlight, thus the designer should exaggerate its scale.

Furthermore, the Architect should reference the symbol keyed to a legend. The symbols when paired (keyed) to a legend may show certain information like the type, property, manufacturer's details and installation details of the particular system. The RCP is also useful to help check on the ceiling appearance and helps the Electrical Engineer to prepare the lighting plan.

- Gridlines and gridlines dimensions to be shown on all drawings
- Room names and numbers
- Section lines
- Callouts for layouts and assembly drawings (if any)

- Ceiling grilles, fixture and ceiling services
- Ceiling levels
- Set-out dimensions and tilling directions
- Specification notes
- Legend

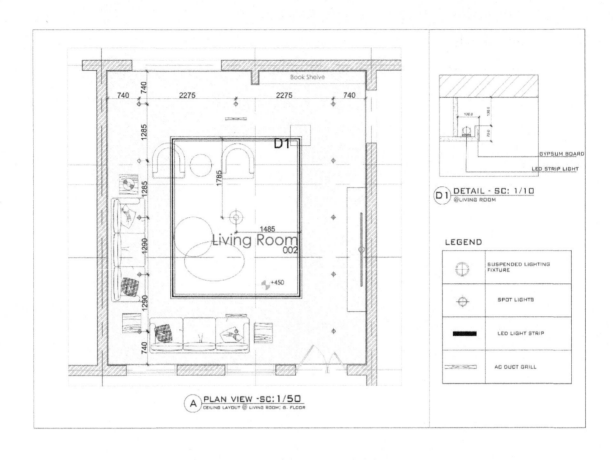

Figure 38: Reflected Ceiling Plan (RCP)

The most important part of a ceiling plan is the dimensions and details. There are many types of materials that can be used to design a ceiling. For instance,

- Wood
- Painting (exposed industrial ceiling)
- Stretched fabric
- Gypsum Board.

Let's consider the Gypsum board ceiling details and plans.

The Gypsum board is also known as Drywall or Plasterboard. Gypsum board can be used for ceiling, walls, and partition systems in residential, commercial and retail projects.

Gypsum board is made up of calcium sulfate dehydrate, with or without additives, extruded between thick sheets of facer and backer paper.

Gypsum Board with Lighting- Ceiling Details.

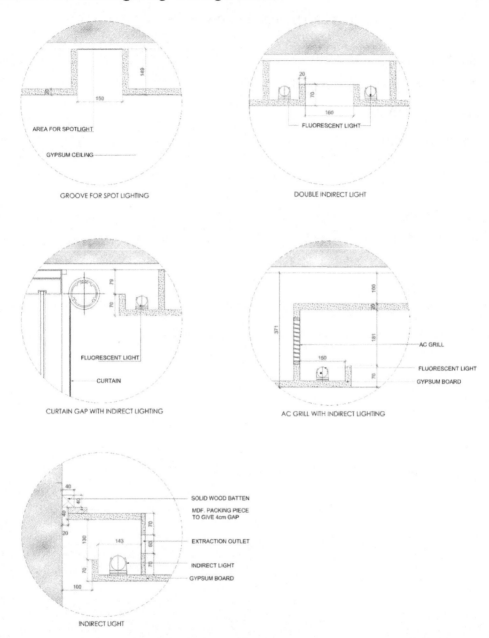

Figure 38: Gypsum Board with Lighting- Ceiling Details

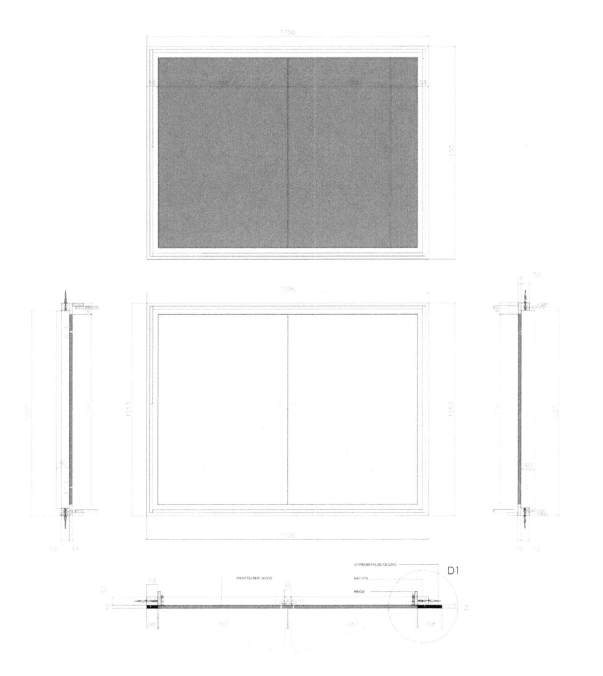

Figure 39a: Access Panel in Gypsum Board Detail

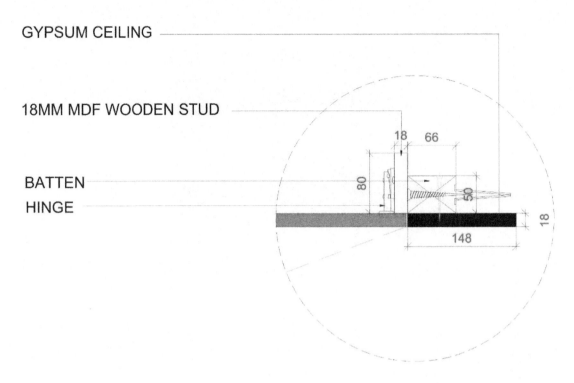

GYPSUM CEILING

18MM MDF WOODEN STUD

BATTEN

HINGE

Figure 39b: Detail 1

3.3.   Roof and Roof Plan

Roofs

The strength of a roof is subject to the characteristics of the material used in its construction and the way in which they are assembled. In essence, roofs are constructed to support its weight, wind pressure, solar panels, snow load and water load. Just as the floor construction is covered with a finishing layer to furnish a smooth, durable and comfortable wearing surface, so the roof construction must be overlaid with finishing to provide a lasting, waterproof and often fireproof cover which will protect the building and its contents. It varies from flat to pitch to other forms that may constitute the wall. The material for its cover includes but is not limited to slates, tiles, shingles, aluminum, iron sheets, P.V.C[14] and so on.

It is a structure covering forming the top of a building. The uppermost part of the building protecting the exterior and interior elements from the hazards of weather. Two types of Roofs: <u>Horizontal</u> (Also known as a flat roof (less than 10^0)) and <u>Pitched</u> (above 10^0).

Roof Terminologies

Span: - Horizontal distance between the internal faces of walls supporting the roof.

Rise: - Vertical height measured from the lowest to the highest point

Run: - Half of the span.

Rafters: - Also called spars. They are diagonals running from the cap to the wall plate. The distance apart depends on the covering materials. The lower

Covering: - External mat laid off fixed on a roof to protect the building.

Wall plate: - They are imbedded in the overlying wall to receive the joists and form a solid bed for the members. It helps transfer the load of the members horizontally throughout the wall. They are held to the wall by stirrups or wall ties.

Pitch: - It is slope angle to the horizontal $= \dfrac{\text{Rise}}{\text{Span}} = \theta$

Ridge: - It is fixed at the highest point to receive the rafter head and king post.

Ridge cap: - It is the ridge covering with a roofing membrane.

Jack Rafters: - They are short spars running from a hip to the eave or from a ridge

---

[14] Polyvinyl Chloride

to a valley

Hip: - It is the line produced when two roof surfaces intersect to form an external angle which is > 180.

Valley: - It is formed by the intersection of two roof surfaces having an external angle which is < 180^0.

Verge: - This is the edge of a roof running from eaves to ridge at a gable end.

Trusses: - They are structural braces supporting rafters and purlins in the absence of cross walls.

Tie Beam: - Horizontal load distributor especially between walls.

King post: Vertical roof member running from tie beam to ridge at the highest level of the roof.

Struts or Noggins small members attached to the tie beam for carrying the ceiling board.

Chimney stack: - Outlet for kitchen and hearth fumes.

Fascia or cladding: - External material used in hiding the roof members and protect them from the hazard of weather.

Purlins: - They are horizontal ties for the rafter and for carrying roof covering.

Truss: - A structure composed of a combination of members that are horizontal, diagonal and vertical forming a rigid framework.

Strut: - A brace, in a vertical, diagonal or horizontal position, used to counter the thrust experienced in a structure.

Noggins: - Used in securing ceiling boards in place.

Cubicle: - A very small enclosed space.

Roof Plan

Roof crowns the building. The design and roof covering help to accentuate the style and design philosophy of the architect. The durability of the structural and covering membrane should be of utmost importance than any other consideration in roofing.

- The roof plan is a drawing that shows the style of roofing to be used for the building. It is usually done in two dimensions. The roof plan must show every item that is necessary to prepare a bid for the roofing contract, such as the size, length and material of fascia and trim board, position of roof vents, flashing profiles, etc. This will help during the bidding process because it makes clear all that the contractor must provide for during the construction.
- Indicate the fall of the roof membrane with arrows on all sides.
- Show the section lines as they appeared on the plan.
- Show all roof gutters, spouts, parapet walls, ducts, chimneys, lightning arrestors, toilet vents, and overhead tanks as they appear.
- Gridlines should be shown as they appear on the plan.
- Open a part of the roof to show the pattern of the noggin, joist and roof members (that is the roof structure arrangement).
- Indicate the type and material for roof covering.
- North point must be shown on all plans (can be shown on the drawing panel)
- Indicate Roof levels

- Call out for layouts and assembly drawings
- Show legend if need be

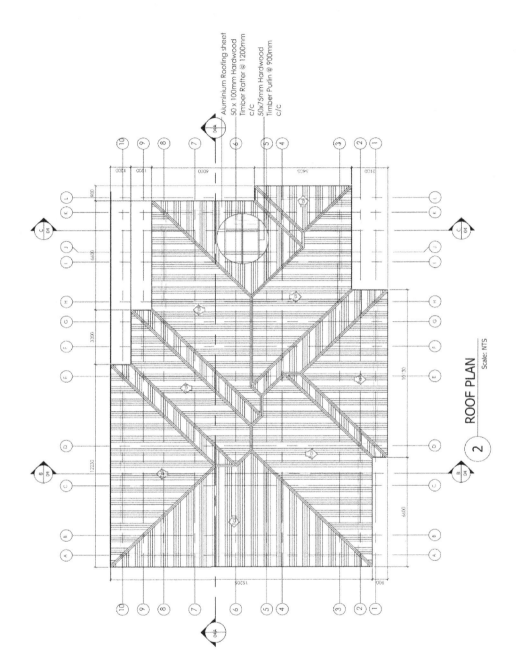

Aluminium Roofing sheet
50 x 100mm Hardwood
Timber Rafter @ 1200mm c/c
50x75mm Hardwood
Timber Purlin @ 900mm c/c

ROOF PLAN
Scale: NTS

2

Figure 40: Showing a Typical Roof Plan

129

3.4. Section

The section is a plane cut through a building (from the top and beyond the nominal ground floor level). It is a drawing that shows the interior features including the roof, helps to describe the method of construction, structural conditions of existing buildings, etc. The types of the section include structural section, detail section, and wall section.

It provides an x-ray of the structure, which helps to clarify possible grey areas in the design. The section lines must cut through all parts of the drawing that will appear in the sectional drawing. In sectional drawings, foundation type used must be shown without specifying the actual depth (this is for the Structural Engineer to decide). The presentation drawing section may avoid showing the foundation details. Any wall or element where the section line cuts through will appear in the graphical representation of that material, and the line representing the element(s) will be highlighted.

Other parts of the drawing facing the cut area will appear in elevation with little or no rendering. If necessary, always introduce anthropometric elements (human figures, trees, cars) to give a feel of the actual scale, but where trees or shrubs are used it is expected that the architect gives details of the type of plant and show relative dimensions at a particular stage of the plant's growth. In sectional drawings, the following should be shown:

- All spaces must be named. Vertical, horizontal and angular dimensions are required on the sectional drawings.
- Any change in the level must be shown.
- Specification write-ups are required.
- In drawing the roof members, you should use roof conventional signs, making sure that they are to scale in relation to the wall thickness.

- Indicate the room levels from where the section lines pass through.
- The space names of all the rooms should be shown.
- Indicate the floor finish, wall finish, ceiling types, roofing type, roof members, roof flashing or gutter and wall skirting (which often the reference is in the schedule for the finish, but reference must be made for it).
- Dimension floor to ceiling height. Dimension floor to lintel height. Dimension floor to the window sill. Dimension height and width of wardrobes, shelves, alcoves, railings, lockers, niche, counters, dividers, thread, risers, balustrade, and so on. Dimension thickness of walls, slabs, cantilevers, etc.
- Also, the gridlines should be shown on the drawing and gridlines dimensions
- Callouts for layouts and assembly drawings
- State the type of roofing sheet, ceiling, and roof trusses

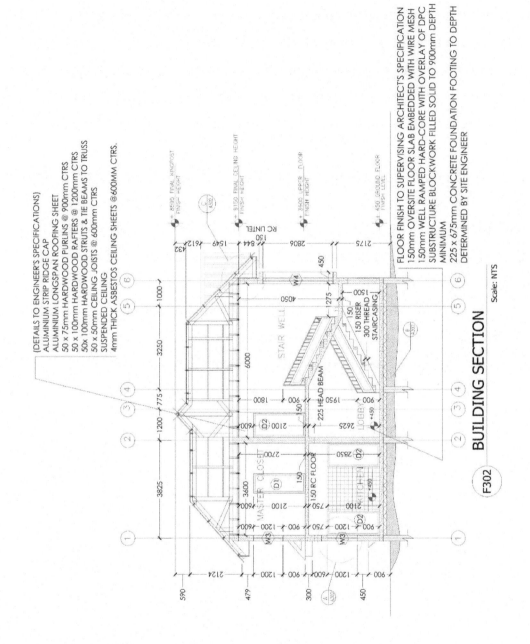

BUILDING SECTION

F302

Scale: NTS

Figure 41a: Sectional Drawing

132

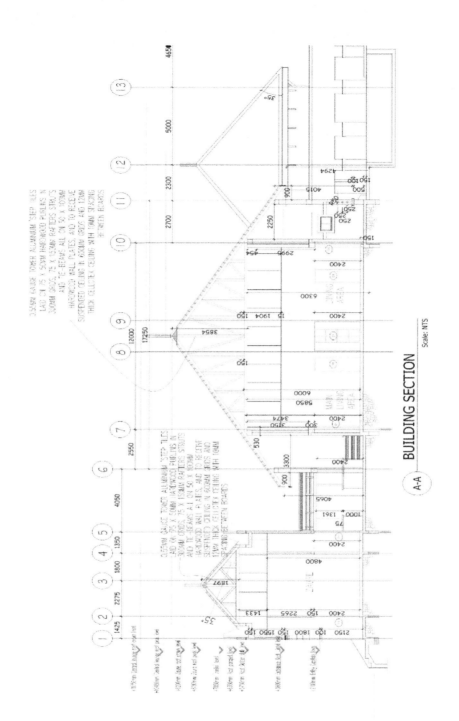

BUILDING SECTION

A-A

Scale: NTS

133

3.5. Elevations

It is the pictorial representation of how the multi-lines in the design will turn out. In practical terms, the designer may adhere to the traditional conventions when making elevations or decide to delve away from these canonical trends. Whatever choice is made depends on the building type, client's likes, statutory requirements, and functionality issues.

- Rendering on the elevation should be reduced or may be avoided completely.
- In cases of change in level and placement, light shadow effects can be used to differentiate the positions of elements.
- If anthropometric elements will be used as the tree and shrubs, the type of tree or shrub should be indicated, dimensions and distances between the tree and shrubs should be indicated. Other major details about the plant type should be included in the landscape schedule.
- Indicate fixed, sliding, openable windows and doors.
- Indicate the overall height of the building.
- Indicate the height of the roof and the height of the wall.
- The various elements (such as windows, doors, bricks) on the elevation must appear in their right architectural symbol as they will appear in reality.
- Elevations are labeled using the cardinal points (East, West, South and North) rather than using Left Side, Right Side, Back Elevation.
- Gridlines and dimensions to be shown on all drawings
- Floor datum
- Window tags
- Curtain wall Tags and door tags
- Specification keynotes
- Callouts for layouts and assembly drawings

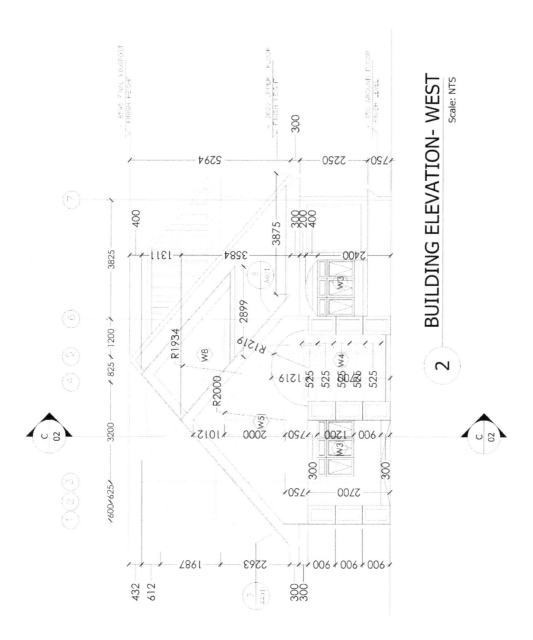

BUILDING ELEVATION- WEST

Scale: NTS

Figure 42: Building Elevation -

135

Interior Elevation

- Gridlines and dimensions to be shown on all drawings
- Floor datum
- Room names and numbers
- Ungraded site level
- Window, door and curtain wall tags
- Set out dimensions for fittings, finishes and fixtures
- Specification keynotes
- Callouts for layouts and assembly drawings
- Legends

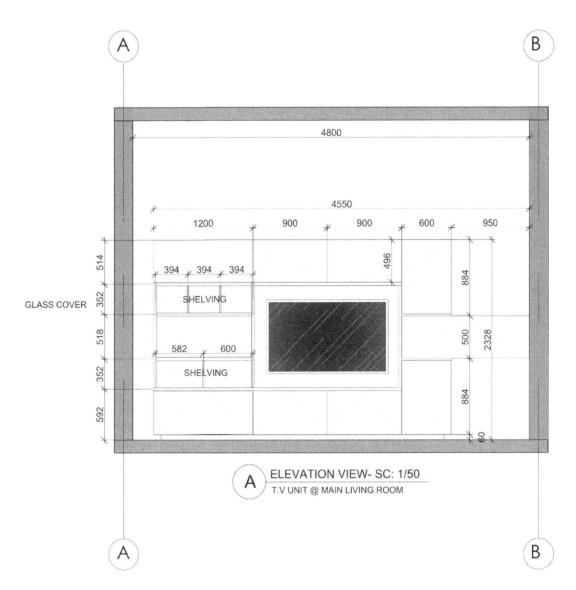

Figure 43a: Interior Elevation

137

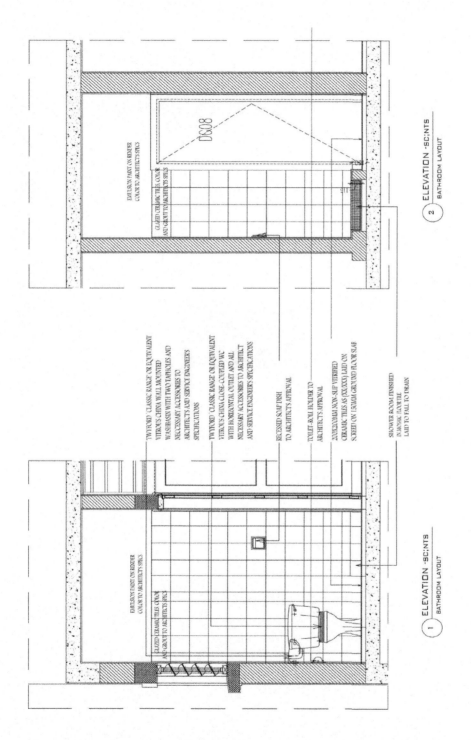

Figure 43b: Interior Elevation

3.6.   Detail Drawings

Detail drawings usually spring up from sectional drawings or any other drawing as the case may be. Detail Drawings are blow-up or magnifying of a part(s) or possible grey areas in a drawing. The dimensions and scale to be used in the blow-up are very important. They are used to explain some of the features which appeared on the drawings that require further clarification. In attempting to detail a specific area, the designer may discover an impossible or unworkable space, angle, or element before the bidding or construction commences. Details help to improve drawing and dimension accuracy. More areas to be detailed may be discovered in the course of detailing work. Usually, areas to be detailed are circled and named like **DD**. The extent of the circle around the element is usually the limit to which the detail will be drawn, nothing more nothing less. A detail spot can be shown on plan, elevation and section. Details should be in a typical working drawing and presentation drawing. Depending on the type of project, architectural detailing needs to be separate from the structural detailing. In any architectural work, detail drawings should not be less than two. Detail drawing can be used to show the manhole, septic tank, soak-away, roof, parapet wall, and any other part of the structure.

- Poor working drawing with missing details can force bids to be unnecessarily high, in the same way, lack of sufficient details in the drawings, regarding project requirements can result in a bid that is too low. Sometimes, details are unnecessarily expensive in terms of their practicality in the field, time factor and cost-effectiveness. Some details suggest a lack of thought as to how the parts will be assembled on site.
- Show details for all elements to be constructed.
- Provide a section for all wall types. When using two wall finishes in one area, show where each finish starts and ends.

- Verify that the details in the drawing coincide with the materials specified and vice-versa.
- Verify that all vents, chimneys, skylights, atriums are included because they are omitted sometimes in the drawings.
- List ceiling height for every room. It is usually written close to the finish schedule.
- Most times, specific details can be obtained from the manufacturer's system description catalogue.

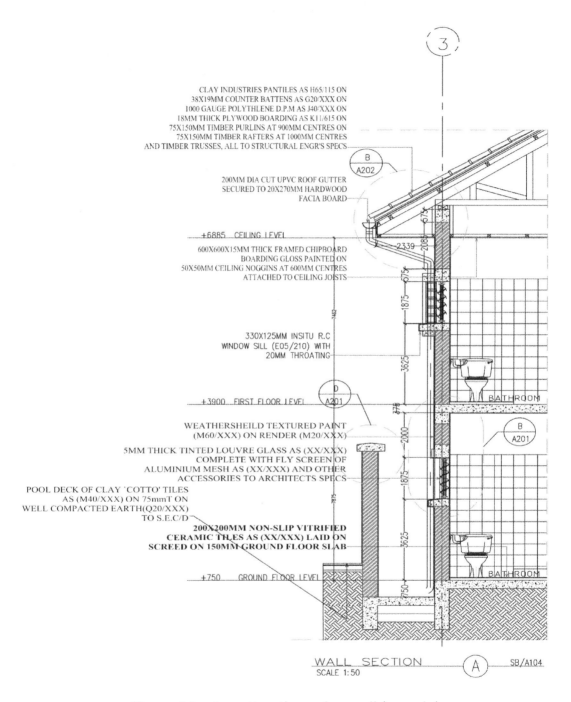

CLAY INDUSTRIES PANTILES AS H65/115 ON
38X19MM COUNTER BATTENS AS G20/XXX ON
1000 GAUGE POLYTHLENE D.P.M AS J40/XXX ON
18MM THICK PLYWOOD BOARDING AS K11/615 ON
75X150MM TIMBER PURLINS AT 900MM CENTRES ON
75X150MM TIMBER RAFTERS AT 1000MM CENTRES
AND TIMBER TRUSSES, ALL TO STRUCTURAL ENGR'S SPECS

B
A202

200MM DIA CUT UPVC ROOF GUTTER
SECURED TO 20X270MM HARDWOOD
FACIA BOARD

+6885   CEILING LEVEL

600X600X15MM THICK FRAMED CHIPBOARD
BOARDING GLOSS PAINTED ON
50X50MM CEILING NOGGINS AT 600MM CENTRES
ATTACHED TO CEILING JOISTS

330X125MM INSITU R.C
WINDOW SILL (E05/210) WITH
20MM THROATING

BATHROOM

+3900   FIRST FLOOR LEVEL

D
A201

WEATHERSHEILD TEXTURED PAINT
(M60/XXX) ON RENDER (M20/XXX)

B
A201

5MM THICK TINTED LOUVRE GLASS AS (XX/XXX)
COMPLETE WITH FLY SCREEN OF
ALUMINIUM MESH AS (XX/XXX) AND OTHER
ACCESSORIES TO ARCHITECTS SPECS

POOL DECK OF CLAY 'COTTO' TILES
AS (M40/XXX) ON 75mmT ON
WELL COMPACTED EARTH(Q20/XXX)
TO S.E.C/D

**200X200MM NON-SLIP VITRIFIED
CERAMIC TILES AS (XX/XXX) LAID ON
SCREED ON 150MM GROUND FLOOR SLAB**

BATHROOM

+750   GROUND FLOOR LEVEL

WALL SECTION
SCALE 1:50

A   SB/A104

Figure 44a: A section through a wall (sample)

141

Assuming we draw the details as shown on the wall sections

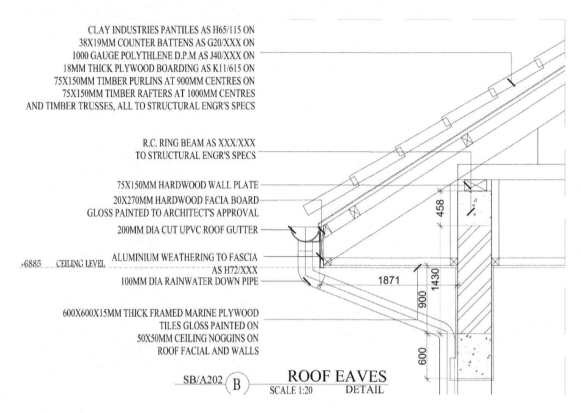

CLAY INDUSTRIES PANTILES AS H65/115 ON
38X19MM COUNTER BATTENS AS G20/XXX ON
1000 GAUGE POLYTHLENE D.P.M AS J40/XXX ON
18MM THICK PLYWOOD BOARDING AS K11/615 ON
75X150MM TIMBER PURLINS AT 900MM CENTRES ON
75X150MM TIMBER RAFTERS AT 1000MM CENTRES
AND TIMBER TRUSSES, ALL TO STRUCTURAL ENGR'S SPECS

R.C. RING BEAM AS XXX/XXX
TO STRUCTURAL ENGR'S SPECS

75X150MM HARDWOOD WALL PLATE
20X270MM HARDWOOD FACIA BOARD
GLOSS PAINTED TO ARCHITECT'S APPROVAL
200MM DIA CUT UPVC ROOF GUTTER

+6885   CEILING LEVEL   ALUMINIUM WEATHERING TO FASCIA
AS H72/XXX
100MM DIA RAINWATER DOWN PIPE

600X600X15MM THICK FRAMED MARINE PLYWOOD
TILES GLOSS PAINTED ON
50X50MM CEILING NOGGINS ON
ROOF FACIAL AND WALLS

SB/A202 (B)   ROOF EAVES
SCALE 1:20   DETAIL

458   1871   1430   900   600

Figure 44b: Detail at B/ A202

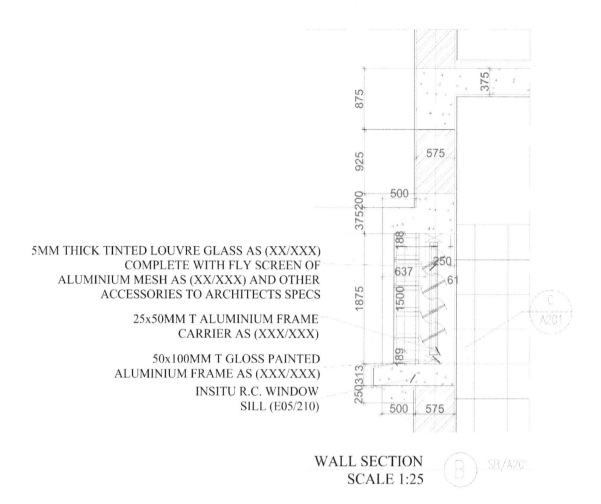

5MM THICK TINTED LOUVRE GLASS AS (XX/XXX)
COMPLETE WITH FLY SCREEN OF
ALUMINIUM MESH AS (XX/XXX) AND OTHER
ACCESSORIES TO ARCHITECTS SPECS

25x50MM T ALUMINIUM FRAME
CARRIER AS (XXX/XXX)

50x100MM T GLOSS PAINTED
ALUMINIUM FRAME AS (XXX/XXX)
INSITU R.C. WINDOW
SILL (E05/210)

WALL SECTION
SCALE 1:25

Figure 44c: Detail Drawing at B/A201

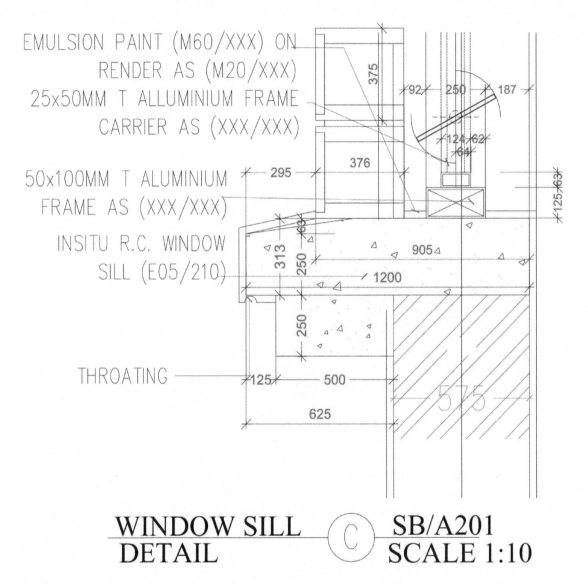

EMULSION PAINT (M60/XXX) ON
RENDER AS (M20/XXX)
25x50MM T ALLUMINIUM FRAME
CARRIER AS (XXX/XXX)

50x100MM T ALUMINIUM
FRAME AS (XXX/XXX)

INSITU R.C. WINDOW
SILL (E05/210)

THROATING

375
92 250 187
124 62
64
295 376
905
1200
313 250
125 63
250
125 500
625
575

WINDOW SILL DETAIL — C — SB/A201 — SCALE 1:10

Figure 44d: Detail Drawing at C/A201

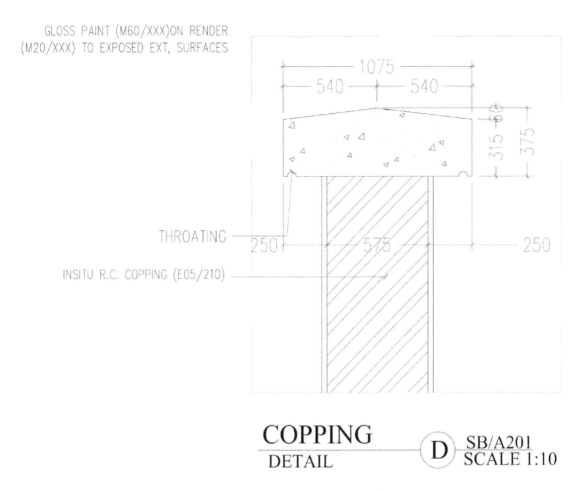

GLOSS PAINT (M60/XXX)ON RENDER
(M20/XXX) TO EXPOSED EXT, SURFACES

THROATING

INSITU R.C. COPPING (E05/210)

COPPING
DETAIL

(D) SB/A201
SCALE 1:10

Figure 44e: Detail Drawing at D/A201

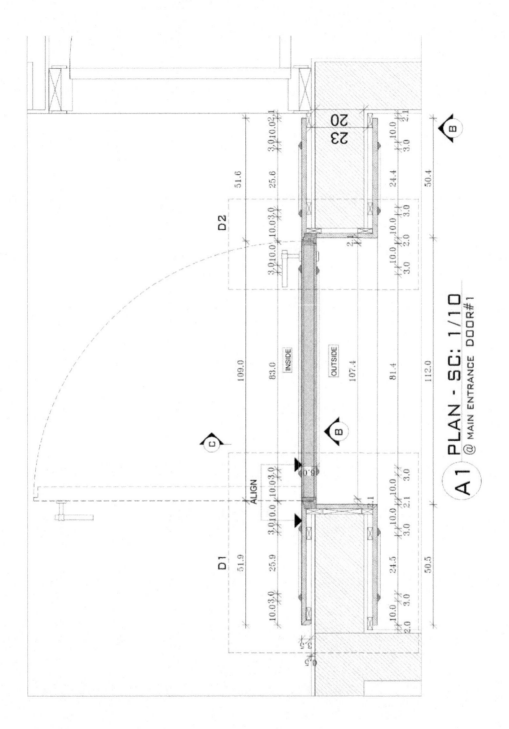

A1 PLAN - SC: 1/10
@ MAIN ENTRANCE DOOR#1

Figure 44f: Classic Door Details A

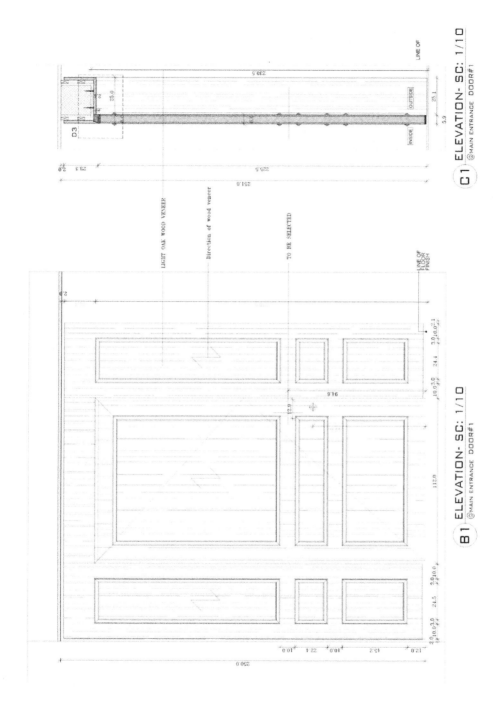

Figure 44f: Classic Door Details B

147

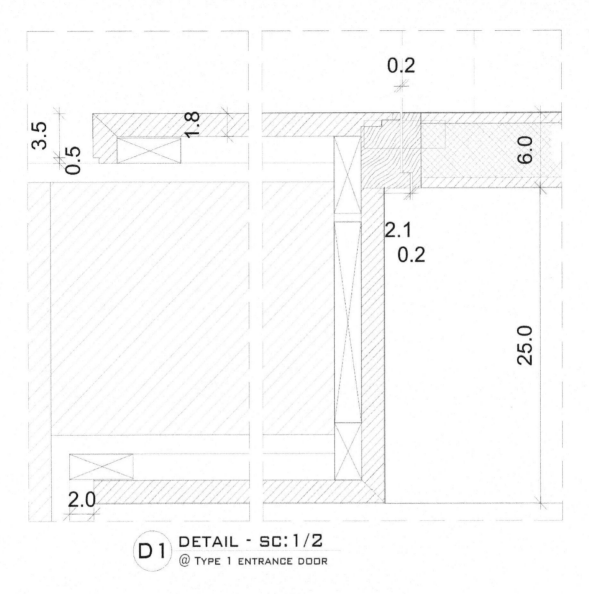

D1 DETAIL - SC:1/2
@ TYPE 1 ENTRANCE DOOR

Figure 44g: Details @Classic Door Details

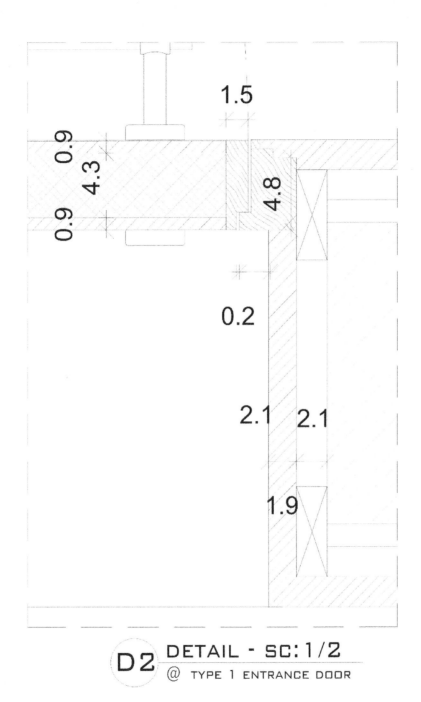

1.5

0.9 0.9

4.3

4.8

0.9

0.2

2.1   2.1

1.9

D2 DETAIL - SC:1/2
@ TYPE 1 ENTRANCE DOOR

Figure 44h: Details @Classic Door Details

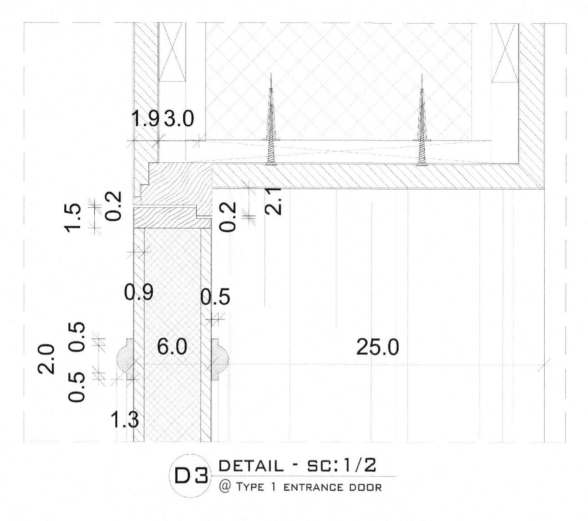

Figure 44i: Details @Classic Door Details

N: B.

The arrangement of these drawings follows an order that is fairly constant. A checklist usually in a tabular format can be used by the architect to assess his work and ensure that omissions and errors are reduced to the minimum. The completeness of drawings almost eliminates guess works, too many questions and saves time (from the bidding stage to the construction time).

A working drawing is also a time to verify the standard of the design. In any case, quality should not be sacrificed for aesthetic goods. As part of being extra sure that the drawings are complete, a visitation to the site may give clues to possible items that may have been omitted in the drawing. On new sites, geotechnical (quality control) testing should be done to eliminate change orders resulting from unknown conditions. It is advisable to have a third party not involved with the project, review the drawings before the final drawing production for the bidding stage. If the job requires that a consultant will make an input to the drawing, the architect must ensure that he reviews it with a clear understanding of all the intents of the consultant otherwise conflict may arise.

3.7. Schedules

These are extra drawings prepared by the architect to show the types, styles, sizes, and any special features when there is more than one particular type of element in a drawing, e.g. window and door schedule, finish, furniture, landscape schedule and so on. Schedules are a convenient method for listing variable conditions. In schedules, we show the sizes (length, width and height) of elements. You should also state the number of elements required for the building. The schedule will also indicate the position of the element in the building. Schedules should be unambiguous, complete and easy to read.

Window Schedule

As referenced on the location plan, the window schedule is meant to show such vital information like the properties of the window (material and type, unit size), the quantity required, manufacturer, type of finish, etc. It is normal to notice a simple reference tag for the window as seen in the floor plan in figure 45 but that is a child`s play for large and complex structures that may have multiple varieties of windows and usually represented with differs unique codes.

Window schedule may show such information as the section of the window type, depending on the scale of the work.

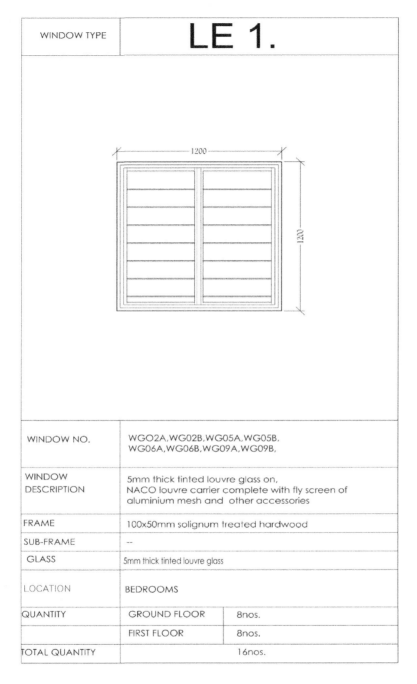

WINDOW TYPE	LE 1.	
WINDOW NO.	WGO2A,WG02B,WG05A,WG05B, WG06A,WG06B,WG09A,WG09B,	
WINDOW DESCRIPTION	5mm thick tinted louvre glass on, NACO louvre carrier complete with fly screen of aluminium mesh and other accessories	
FRAME	100x50mm solignum treated hardwood	
SUB-FRAME	--	
GLASS	5mm thick tinted louvre glass	
LOCATION	BEDROOMS	
QUANTITY	GROUND FLOOR	8nos.
	FIRST FLOOR	8nos.
TOTAL QUANTITY	16nos.	

Figure 45: A typical window schedule

Door Schedule

This should contain information such as quantity required, size, type of door, material and remarks. More detailed information such as frame type, hardware, and fire rating, is generally required for large commercial projects

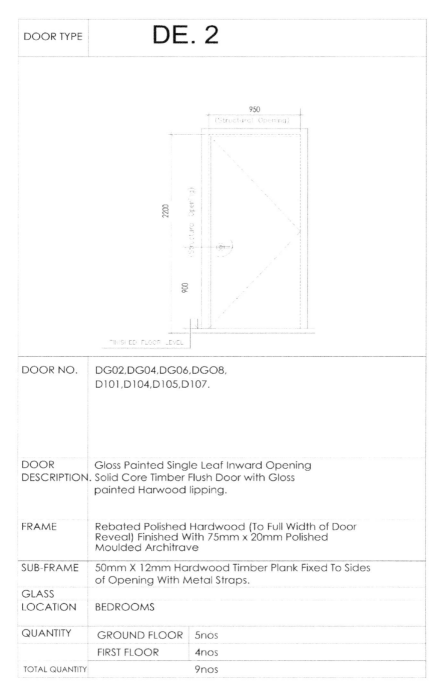

DOOR TYPE	DE. 2	
DOOR NO.	DG02,DG04,DG06,DGO8, D101,D104,D105,D107.	
DOOR DESCRIPTION.	Gloss Painted Single Leaf Inward Opening Solid Core Timber Flush Door with Gloss painted Harwood lipping.	
FRAME	Rebated Polished Hardwood (To Full Width of Door Reveal) Finished With 75mm x 20mm Polished Moulded Architrave	
SUB-FRAME	50mm X 12mm Hardwood Timber Plank Fixed To Sides of Opening With Metal Straps.	
GLASS		
LOCATION	BEDROOMS	
QUANTITY	GROUND FLOOR	5nos
	FIRST FLOOR	4nos
TOTAL QUANTITY	9nos	

Figure 46: A Typical Door Schedule

155

Finish Schedule

We could use two methods to describe this too, either using the room/space number or the code for exact space. For example, the bathroom layout in figure 47a, the space number is 013, for the preliminary schedule we could consider the floor, wall and ceiling finish schedule.

Figure 47a: Bathroom Layout

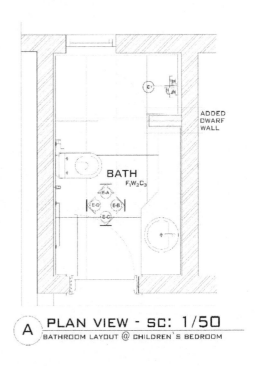

Figure 47b: Bathroom Layout

Concerning the drawing above, the dimensions and some details were not inserted.

FINISH SCHEDULE

ROOM		FLOOR	SKIRTING	WALLS				CEILING	REMARKS
No.	NAME			NORTH (N)	EAST (E)	WEST (W)	SOUTH (S)		
013	Bathroom	EBN713 9.2mm Thick Sybaris 43 x 43 Ceniza	-	DYB713 10.2mm Thick Sybaris 31 x 60 Ceniza	DYB713 10.2mm Thick Sybaris 31 x 60 Ceniza	EFN670 10.2mm Thick Delfas 31 x 60 Marfil	DYB713 10.2mm Thick Sybaris 31 x 60 Ceniza	600x600x15 mm Acoustic Mineral Fibre Suspended Ceiling Tiles on Aluminium Grid	

Table 4a: Room Finish Schedule

In the table above we made some assumptions, first we assumed that the north side of the bathroom is indicated, 'A', Southside, 'C', Eastside, 'D' and Westside, 'B'. Secondly, we made the assumption that the tiles selection was from, SALONI[15] catalogue.

For the walls, sometimes the wall finish for one is different from another, when that is the case, the architect can use the North, East, South and West to indicate the type of finish on each wall.

Assuming the bedroom had the code F1, S1, W1, and C1 representing the floor, skirting, wall and ceiling respectively as seen in figure 47b, we can then prepare a simple room finish like the one seen below.

---

[15] *https://www.saloni.com/en*

FINISH SCHEDULE

ROOM		FLOOR (F1)	SKIRTING (S1)	WALLS (W2)				CEILING	REMARKS
No.	NAME			NORTH (N)	EAST (E)	WEST (W)	SOUTH (S)		
013	Bathroom	EBN713 9.2mm Thick Sybaris 43 x 43 Ceniza	-	DYB713 10.2mm Thick Sybaris 31 x 60 Ceniza	EFN670 10.2mm Thick Delfas 31 x 60 Marfil	DYB713 10.2mm Thick Sybaris 31 x 60 Ceniza	DYB713 10.2mm Thick Sybaris 31 x 60 Ceniza	600x600x15 mm Acoustic Mineral Fibre Suspended Ceiling Tiles on Aluminium Grid	

Table 4b: Room Finish Schedule

3.8. Specification

As the name implies, it is a standard architectural write-up or instructions indicating or specifying the precise or range of materials and brand of products to be used in the construction of the building, e.g. Use Berger paint number 30-40 for all the interior spaces. It is a project manual that is used in a site to explain the construction details. They are graphic notations, written notes, pictures, dimensions and so on.

The specification has become so important because projects are getting more complex. There is a general realization that a thorough specification meant a reduced cost of construction and unlikely assumptions by other tradesmen. Also, litigation problems are reduced when proper specifications are made. They are read by the Builder's Estimator, by the Quantity Surveyor, by the Clerk of Work and the Builder's Foreman during the progress of the contract. In small projects, it is read in conjunction with the working drawing as the only basis for tendering by contractors. In large projects, it is given to the Quantity Surveyor together with the working drawings for production of the bill of quantities (B.Q). Specifications come as notes in drawings and are sometimes written (technical specification) on separate booklets. They can be accompanied with pictures or sketches of the product or construction technique. Duplications experienced in writing drawing notes and actual specifications should be reduced to the minimum. While notes help to locate the position, placement, item and size, the full specification will include more information like the manufacturer, manual and other relevant information that will assist in installation, use and maintenance. Room-finish notes must not be in conflict with the specification write-up. In such a case, the specification write-up supercedes the former, else verification from the designer or specifier is required. Specification write-up is divided into two parts: The **technical aspect** (deals with materials) and the **non-technical aspect** (deals with various contract clauses).

Specification helps the builders in maintaining a set quality and quantity of material and finishing and instructions on how to handle them. It acts as a guide in construction work, to help Project Supervisors meet with a required standard. It conveys extra information that cannot be easily explained with only drawings.

In specification write-up, the specifier must comply with government authority guidelines for various items and products but the specifier is responsible for the final decisions he makes and any problems caused by reliance on them. It is always very important that even before the conceptual stage early contact with the code authority should be made as this will help direct the architect along the path that will ensure he meets with those standards.

- It is good practice to reconcile specifications with drawings to reduce conflict.
- Avoid including a specification that doesn't apply to the project to reduce confusion. In short, specification should be "*specific*" to allow bidders to know exactly what to bid for. Even in cases where the manufacturer has only one product, he usually has a name for it and if so should be written.
- In the specification, avoid including equipment because they don't require any special installation e.g. refrigerators, television, photocopying machines, etc.
- The specifier must ensure that items like windows, doors, finishings are completely scheduled to reduce the number and ambiguity of items to be specified.
- Avoid specifying products that are obsolete, not available or no longer in use. It behoves on the specifier to be abreast with the latest trends.

- It is also very important that one should keep in mind the availability of materials for maintenance when specifying materials, equipment and technique.

- The specification must be prepared specifically for the project. It is misleading to use generic specifications for all similar projects because it leaves a lot of unanswered questions about the peculiarity of this current project. In some instances, especially on projects that have many documents, detail sheets sometimes show a cursory review of the details with the on-applicable details crossed out. These non-applicable details and specification that are crossed out create added drawings which are unnecessary and make the paperwork cumbersome.

- Ensure that you indicate in the specification the tradesmen to install your equipment because confusion sometimes arises e.g. mechanical and electrical contractors may have problems with who will install the control wiring for HVAC (heating, ventilation and air conditioning) equipment.

- The working drawings and specification must exactly describe the scope and details of such alternative bids and their ramifications should be separately placed in each section of the relevant specification.

There are **Six** types of specification:

1. Performance Specification: This is when the architect is considering the capability of the material e.g. using the elevator with a capacity to carry 150 people per hour, a two horsepower air conditioner, a 60-decibel sound system, etc.

2. Descriptive Specification: It is when a total explanation of the product is given e.g. use an air condition using 220volts, ¼ horsepower, and motor supported by a rigid frame attached to firm support.

3. Brand name Specification: The material is specified using the manufacturer's name e.g. 600mm by 600mm Emenite ceiling boards.
4. Closed Specification: The product is specified using a particular model number or a particular manufacturer's product or a range of models e.g.640BDC, 600mm by 600mm Emenite ceiling boards. It does not give room for choice by the contractor.
5. Open Specification: It is used when most manufacturers' products meet the required standard. It is a combination of performance and descriptive specifications. In this, the contractor is left with a choice of selecting from a range of products that fall under that category.
6. Reference Specification: The product is specified by referring to a number published on a catalogue or journal e.g. the terrazzo tiles shall conform with the Nigerian Standard Organization number, TZ-11023-E.

In the specification, one should avoid repetition or duplication, i.e. information gotten from drawings need not be repeated in specification write-up. Before you can properly specify, it is necessary to know the material property in order to establish its limitations. Use clear technical and precise language in specification to avoid creating confusion. The simpler the language, the better. Avoid any legal ambiguities when using formal sentences in specification write-up. Good specification writing should have minimum errors, should be easy to use, and should have minimum omissions and inconsistencies.

Chapter Four

DATA SOURCES AND USEFUL INFORMATION

4.0. National Building Code

The building code is set of rules that specify the minimum standards for buildings and non-building structures of a particular jurisdiction which becomes a law only after it has been enacted by the appropriate authority (governmental or private authority) of that jurisdiction. The building codes differ from country to country and may be referred to as the 'National Building Code' as it is also called in Nigeria.

Normally for its preparation, stakeholders in the building industry are contacted for their input. These stakeholders may include professionals in the building industry (Architects, Builders, Engineers, Estate Surveyors and Valuators, Quantity surveyors, Land Surveyors, Urban and Regional Planners). These codes when enacted become a law that is essential to help in planning towns and cities, curb incessant collapse of buildings, fire infernos, built environment abuse, use of non-professionals and quacks, use of untested products and materials and so on.

The scope of the building code is usually wide and covers a variety of items. It touches issues that relate to standards for structures and specific building uses, rules regarding parking, fire codes to minimize the risk of fire and safety standards in case of fire, allowable installation methodologies and so on. For example, the National Building Code of the Federal Republic of Nigeria is divided into parts

Part I - *Administration (Section 1-3)*

Part II - *Classifications and Requirements (*Sections 4 and 5) Sections 6-12 stipulates the requirements from the major stakeholders with reference to the *working tools* from Sections 4 and 5.

Part III - forms the *Enforcement* part of the Codes. The entire Building Process is divided into four (4) convenient stages and developed under two (2) subheadings:

- Pre-Design Stage - Requirements and Enforcement;
- Design Stage - Requirements and Enforcement;
- Construction Stage - Requirements and Enforcement; and
- Post-Construction Stage - Requirements and Enforcement.

Part IV – *Schedules;* where all *supportive documents, data, tables, information* and all sorts of *relevant* and *approved application forms* to *Part I, II, and III* can be found[16].

Thus, every architect who wishes to practice in Nigeria must **study**, **understand** and **apply** it, for it is an essential guide to design standards.

4.1. CSI Master Format

MasterFormat is a general method of organizing project manuals and documents under categories using the standardized guidelines to relate drawings to specifications for every commercial, industrial and residential project in the world. It provides established guidelines applicable to almost all construction documents, contracts and drawings. MasterFormat is a product of the Construction

---

[16] National Building Code of the Federal Republic of Nigeria

Specifications Institute (CSI) and Construction Specifications Canada (CSC).

CSI MasterFormat is divided into sections and numbers that help professionals (Project owners, Architects, Contractors, Suppliers, etc.) organize construction requirements, products, specifications and activities by groups or trades.

4.2. NBS Specifications.

The National Building Specification, and now known as the NBS, is a UK-based system of construction specification used by architects and other building professionals to describe the materials, standards and workmanship of a construction project. The NBS has been structured on the Common Arrangement of Work Sections.

4.3. Building Maintenance Manual

It is a post-construction document written (using the material provided by the client and following standards procedures in use) and issued by the Architect to the client and the occupier of the building for the smooth running, control and maintenance of all the elements, fixtures and spaces in the building. It helps to prolong the lifetime of the structure and decreases harmful interruptions in use and building occupation. If electronic items and other household equipment bought for just a few thousand nairas can come with a manual, how much more a structure one has expended millions of naira.

4.4. Building Information Modelling (BIM)

The concept of BIM first appeared as early as 1962, when Douglas Engelbart wrote his paper "Augmenting Human Intellect: A conceptual Framework' and describe architect entering specifications and data into a building design and watching a structure take shape- a concept very similar to modern parametric modeling.

BIM is defined by the US National Building Information Modelling Standard as 'a digital representation of physical and functional characteristics of a facility'. It is a technology that displays all vital information about a project digitally that is, the cost, quantities of materials, dimensions, etc. In other words, it is managing all the information on a project before, during and after construction in a holistic and accurate manner.

With BIM collaborations can be established between specialists, for example, architects, engineers and construction professionals who can work in their various areas of expertise without having to wait for one another.

BIM involves the creation of a digital model that contains all parts of a facility together with their features which may include material, weight, soil conditions, etc.

The benefits of BIM are varied they include,

- It provides better design coordination and improved constructability.
- BIM helps to strengthen understanding visually thereby enabling specialists to communicate effectively during the project lifecycle.
- BIM is able to track the types and quantities of materials and enhance the efficient use of them

- It is easy to find out conflicts early in the life of the project and resolve them, thus BIM helps reduce conflicts and changes during construction.
- It greatly saves time used in carrying out the project especially on an activity like drafting which is very time consuming, thereby saving costs. Quantities and data can be automatically generated by the model, producing estimates and workflows much more quickly than conventional processes.

Appendix 1.   Working Drawing Abbreviations

$	and	A.P.	access panel
&	and	A/C	air conditioning
"L"	angle	ABV	above
<	angle	AC	acoustical
</	angle	ACC	access
@	at	ACC	accessory
/	by	ACI	American Concrete
c (	centerline		Institute
[	channel	ACOUS	acoustical
o	degree	ACOUS BD	acoustical board
0	diameter	ACOUST	acoustical tile
=	equal	AD	access door
(E)	existing	ADD	addendum
'	feet	ADD'L	additional
FL	flow line	ADH	adhesive
'	foot	ADJ	adjacent

"	inch(es)	ADJ	adjustable
#	number	AFF	above finished floor
/	per	AGGR	aggregate
%	percent	AL	aluminum
PL	plate	ALT	alternate
+	plus/minus	ANCH	anchor
#	pound	ANOD	anodized
0	round	APPD	approved
0	square	APPROX	approximate
A.B.	anchor bolt	APPROX	Approximately
A.D.	area drain	ARCH	Architect
A.E.	Architect-engineer	ARCH	Architectural
A.M.H. S	Automatic material	ASB	Asbestos
	handling system	ASPH	Asphalt
ASSOC	Association	C.CONC.	Cast concrete
ASSY	Assembly	C/C	Centre to centre
ATTEN	Attenuation	C.B.	Catch basin
AUTO	Automatic	C.B.	Chalk board

AVER	Average	C.C.G.	Concrete curb and gutter
AWG	American wire gauge	C.F.C.I.	Contractor furnish, contractor install
B.F.	both faces	C.G.	corner guard
B.M.	bench mark	C.I.	cast iron
B.O.	bottom of	C.I.P.	cast iron pipe
B.O.	by others	C.J.	construction joint
B.P.	base plate	C.J.	control joint
B.U.	built –up	C.L.	center line
B.U.R.	built –up roofing	C.L.F.	chain link fence
B.U.R.	built-up roof	C.M.P.	corrugate metal pipe
B.W.	both ways	C.O.	clean out
BATT	battery	C.R.	cold rolled
BB	baseboard	C.R.S.	cold rolled steel
BD	board	C.T.	ceramic tile
BDRM	bedroom	C.W.	cold water
BEL	below	C.W.	concrete walk
BET	between	C/O	cased opening

BEV	beveled	CAB	cabinet
BEY	beyond	CALK	caulk
BITJM	bituminous	CCM	cubic centimeter
BLDG	building	CEM	cement
BLK	block	CEM	cementitious
BLKG	blocking	CEM. PLAS.	cement plaster
BLVD	boulevard	CER	ceramic
BM	beam	CFM	cubic feet per minute
BOT	bottom	CIR	circle
BRG	bearing	CIR	circular
BRK	brick	CIR	circumference
BRKT	bracket	CL. GL	clear glass
BRZ	bronze	CL.W.GL.	clear wire glass
BSMT	basement	CLG	ceiling
BTH	bathroom	CLKG	caulking
BTN	batten	CLO	closet
BVL	bevel	CLR	clear
C	Celsius		

c/c	Centre to Centre	CLR	clearance
C	channel	CLRM	classroom
C	course	CM	cubic meter
CMM	cubic millimeter	D.C.	Drainage conductor
CMU	concrete masonry unit	D.F.	Drinking fountain
		D.H.	Double hung
CNTR	counter	D.L.	Dead load
CO	company	D.O.	Door opening
CO2	carbon dioxide	D.R.	Dressing room
COL	column	D.S.P.	Dry standpipe
COMB	computer	DBL	double
COMPR	compressed	DEG	degree
COMPR	compressor	DEMO	demolition
COMPT	compartment	DEPT	department
CON	conference	DET	detail
CONC	concrete	DIA	diameter
CONC. FL	concrete floor	DIAG	diagonal
COND	condenser	DIAG	diagram

COND	condition	DIAG	diagrammatic
CONN	connect	DIFF	diffuser
CONN	connection	DIM	dimension(s)
CONST	construction	DIM	dispenser
CONT	continue	DIST	distance
CONT	continuous	DISTR	distribute
CONTR	contract	DISTR	distribution
CONTR	contractor	DISTR	distributed
CONV	convector	DIV	divider
COR	corridor	DIV	division
CORR	corrugated	DMBW	dumbwaiter
CPG	coping	DN	down
CPG	copper	DO	ditto
CPT	carpet	DOC	documents
CPT	carpeted	DP	damp proofing
CR	crushed	DP	deep
CSG	casing	DR	door
CSK	countersink	DS	downspout

CSK	countersunk	DW	dishwasher
CSK/S	countersunk Screw	DWG	drawing
		DWR	drawer
CSMT	casement	E	east
CTG	coating	E.TOE.	End to end
CTR	center	E.B.	Expansion bolt
CU	cubic	E.C.	Electrical conduit
CU. FT.	cubic feet	E.C.	Electrical contractor
CY	cubic yard(s)		
E.F.	Each face	F.A.I.	Fresh air intake
E.J.	Expansion joint	F.B.	Face brick
E.P	electric panel	F.B.	Flat bar
E.P.B.	electrical panel board	F.D.	Floor drain
		F.D.C.	Fire department connection
E.W.	each way		
E.W.C.	electric water cooler	F.DR.	Folding door
		F.E.	Fire extinguisher
EA	each	F.E.C.	fire extinguisher

EIFS	exterior insulation		cabinet
	and finish system	F.F.	finish floor
EL	elevation datum	F.F&E.	furniture,
EL	elevation view		furnishings &
ELAST	elastic		equipment
ELAST	elastomeric	F.H.	fire hose
ELB	elbow	F.H.	flat head.
ELEC	electric	F.H.C	fire hose cabinet
ELEC	electrical	F.H.R.	fire hose rack
ELEC. CLO.	electrical closet	F.H.S.	flat head screw
ELEV	elevator	F.JT.	flush joint
EMER	emergency	F.L.	flow line
ENC	enclose	F.O.	face of
ENCL	enclosure	F.O.C.	face of concrete
ENGR	engineer	F.O.F.	face of finish
ENT	entrance	F.O,M.	face of masonry
EQ	equal	F.O.S.	face of studs
EQUIP	equipment	F.S.	far side

EST	estimate	F.S.	full size
EXC	excavate	F.V.	façade view
EXC	excavation	F.V.	face view
EXH	exhaust	FAB	fabricate
EXIST	existing	FAB	fabricated
EXP	expansion	FAB	fabrication
EXPD	exposed	FBD	fiberboard
EXT	extension	FD	fire damper
EXT	exterior	FDN	foundation
F	face	FED	federal
F	Fahrenheit	FH	fire hydrant
F.HYD.	fire to face	FIN	finish
F.A	face alarm	FIXT	fixture
F.A.A.	fire alarm annunciator	FL.CO.	floor cleanout
		FLASH	flashing
FLEX	flexible	GL	glass
FLG	flooring	GL	glazed
FLR	floor	GL	glazing

FLR. MTD.	floor mounted	GL.OPG.	glass opening
FLUOR	fluorescent	GLZ. TILE	glazed tile
FP	flat point	GND	ground
FPM	feet per minute	GOVT	government
FPRF	fireproofing	GR	grade
FPS	feet per second	GYP	gypsum
FR	frame	GYP	gypsum drywall
FR	framed	GYP.BD.	gypsum board
FR	framing	H	high
FT	feet	H.PT.	high point
FT	foot	H.B.	hose bibb
FTG	footing	H.C	hollow core
FUR	furred	H.D	hair dryer
FUR	furring	H.D.F.	handicap drinking
FURN	furnace		fountain
FURN	furnish	H.E.W.C.	handicap electric
FUT	future		water cooler
G	gas	H.H.D.	handicap hair dryer

G.B.	grab bar	H.LAV.	handicap lavatory
G.C.	general contractor	H.M.	hollow metal
		H.MI.	handicap mirror
G.F.	granular fill	H.P.	horse power
G.I.	galvanized iron	H.R.	handrail
G.R.	guardrail	H.S.D.	handicap soap dispenser
G.S.	galvanized steel		
G.W.B.	gypsum wall board	H.S.H.	handicap shower head
G/B/O	gypsum board opening	H.U.	handicap urinal
		H.W.	hot water
GA	gage	H.W.C.	handicap wall-mounted wall closet
GA	gauge		
GAL	gallon	HC	handicap
GALV	galvanizes	HC	handicapped
GD	guard	HD	head
GEN	general	HDBD	hardboard
GEN	generator	HDNR	hardener

181

GFRC	glass fiber	HDR	header Reinforced
HDW	hardware		concrete
HEX	hexagonal	JCT	junction
HK	hooks	JNT	joint
HOR	horizontal	JR	junior
HOSP	hospital	JST	joist
HP	high point	JT	joint
HR	hour	JTS	joints
HT	height	K	kip (1000ibs)
HTG	heating	K. PL.	kick plate
HTR	heater	K.D.	knock down
HVAC	heating,	K.O.	knock out
	Ventilation, and	KW	kilowatt
HVY	heavy	L	length
HWY	highway	L.B.	lag bolt
I.D.	inside diameter	L.CMU	lightweight core
I.D.	interior diameter		masonry unit(s)
I.P.S.	inside pipe size	L.F.	linear foot

IC	intercom	L.G.	lead glass
IMPR	impregnate	L.H.	left hand
IN	inch(es)	L.L.	live load
INC	incorporated	L.L.H.	long leg horizontal
INCAND	incandescent	L.L.V.	long leg vertical
INCIN	incinerate	L.P.	low point
INCL	include	L.RM.	living room
INCL	included	L.W.C.	light weight concrete
INCL	including	LAB	laboratory
IND	industrial	LAD	ladder
INDIV	individual	LAM	laminate
INFO	information	LAV	lavatory
INSL	insulate	LB	pound
INSL	insulating	LIN	linen
INSL	insulation	LKR	locker
INST	install	LOC	location
INT	interior	LT	light
INT	internal	LTL	lintel

INTERM	intermediate	LVR	louver
INV	invert	M	thousand
ISOL	isolate	M.PARTN	movable partition
ISOL	isolation	M.C.	mechanical
IV	intravenous		contractor
J.B.	junction box	M.C.	medicine cabinet
JAN	janitors closet	M.C.	miscellaneous
M.C.	mis channel	MUT	muntin channel
		N	north
M.E.	match existing	N.C.	noncorrosive
M..H.	manhole	N.I.C.	not in contract
M.L.	metal lath	N.S.	near side
M.O.	masonry opening	N.S.	non slip
M.S.	masonry shelf	.T.S.	not to scale
MACH	machine	N$_2$O	nitrous oxide
MACH.RM.	machine room	NARC	narcotics
MAS	masonry	NFPA	national fire
MAS.BLK.	masonry block		protection association

MAT	material	NIP	nipple
MAX	maximum	NO	number
MB	marker board	NOM	nominal
MBR	member	NORM	normal
MECH	mechanical	NRC	noise reduction
MED	medical		coefficient
MED	medium	O.TO O.	out to out
MED.STO.	medications storage	O.C.	on center(s)
MEMB	membrane	O.D.	outside diameter
MEMO	memorandum	O.F.C.I	owner furnish,
MEZZ	mezzanine		contractor
MFD	manufactured	O.F.O.I.	owner furnish,
MFG	manufacture		owner install
MFR	manufacturer	O.F.S.	outside face of
MGR	manager stud		
MIN	minimum	O/	over
MIR	mirror	O2	oxygen
MISC	miscellaneous	OA	overall

MK	mark	OB	obscures
MLDG	moulding	OBS	obsolete
MOD	model	OFF	office
MOD	modular	OH	overhead
MOD	module	OPNG	opening
MON	monitor	OPP	opposite
MON	monument	OPPH	oppositehand
MOV	movable	ORIG	original
MTD	mounted	ORN	ornament
MTG	mounting	OV.H.S	ova lhead screw
MTG.HT.	mounting height	OVHG	overhang
MTL	metal	OWN FURN.	owner furnished
MUL	mullion	OZ	ounce
P	page	PKWY	parkway
P.A.	public address	PL	plate
P.B.	Panic bar	PLAS	plaster
P.C.P.	Portland cement	PLAT	platform
PLT	plaster	PLF	pounds per linear foot
P.C.T.	precast terrazo		
P.G.	plate glass	PLMB	plumbing
P.L.	property line	PLYWD	plywood
P.LAM.	plastic laminate	PNEU	pneumatic

36

186

P.P.GL.	polished plate glass	PNL	panel
		PNLG	paneling
P.R.V.	pressure reducing valve	PNT	paint
		POL	polish
P.S.	plan section	PORT	portable
P.T.	pressure treated	POS	position
P.T.D.	paper towel		
PR	pair dispenser	PRCST	precast concrete
P.T.D/R.	combination paper towel dispenser &	PRD.GYP.	poured gypsum
		PREFAB	prefabricate
P.T.D/R	paper towel	PREFIN	prefinished
		PREP	preparation
P.T.STA	pneumatic tube station	PROD	product
		PROJ	project
P.W.GL	polished wire glass	PROP	property
		PSF	pounds per square foot
PAR	paragraph		
PAR	parallel	PSI	pounds per square

PARA	parapet		inch
PART.BD.	particle board	PT	part
PASS	passage	PT	point
PAT	patent	PT. CRV.	Point of curve
PC	piece	PT.TAN	point of tangency
PC.C	precast concrete	PTD	painted
PCF	pounds	PTN	partition
	foot	PVC	polyvinyl chloride
PED	pedestal	PVC.P	pvp pipe
PERF	perforate	PVMT	pavement
PERF	perforated	PWR	power
PERM	permanent	Q.T.	quarry tile
PERP	perpendicular	Q.T.B.	quarry tile base
PH	phase	Q.T.FLR.	quarry tile floor
PHOTO	photograph	QRY	quarry
QTR.	quarter	S	south
QTY	quantity	S.B.	splash back
R	radius	S.C.	self closing

R	riser	S.C.	sill cock
R.A.	return air	S.C.	solid core
R.B.	rubber base	S.C.D.	seat cover
R.C.	reinforced concrete		
	Pipe	S.C.T.	structural clay tile
R.D.	roof drain	S.D.	soap dispenser
R.H.	right hand	S.D.	storm drain
R.H.R.	right hand reverse	S.F.	square foot
R.O.	rough opening	S.F.	storefront
R.W.L.	rain water leader	S.G.	semi gloss
RAD	radiator	S.G.D.	sliding glass door
RAD	radius	S.H.	shower head
RD	road	S.N.D.	sanitary napkin
RE	refer		dispenser
RECIRC	recirculation	S.N.R.	sanitary napkin
RECOMM	recommendation		receptor
RECP	receptacle	S.P.	starting point
RECT	rectangle	S.S.	sanitary shower

RED	reducer	S.SNK.	service sink
REF	reference	S.V.	sheet vinyl
REFG	refrigerator	S.Y.	square yard
REG	regulator	SAD	saddle
REINF	reinforced	SAN	sanitary
REINF	reinforcement	SC	scale
REINF	reinforcing	SCH	schedule
REPR	repair		
REPRO	reproduce	SCN	screen
REQ	require	SDG	siding
REQD	required	SEAL	sealant
RESIL	resilient	SEC	second
RESIST	resistant	SECT	section
RET	return	SEP	separation
REV	reversed	SERV	service
REV	revise	SF.GL.	safety glass
REV	revision	SFTY	safety
RFG	roofing	SH	shelf

RGTR	register	SHLVG	shelving
RM	room	SHT	sheet
RR	railroad	SHTHG	sheathing
S	sink	SHWR	shower
SIM	similar	SWBD	switchboard
SKL	skylight	SYM	symmetrical
SL	slab	SYN	synthetic
SL	sliding	SYS	system
SMLS	seamless	T	tread
SOF	soffit	T&B	top & bottom
SP.CTG.	special coating	T&G	tongue & groove
SPC	space	T.P.HLDR.	toilet paper holder
SPC	spacer	T.B.	tack board
SPCG	spacing	T.B.	towel bar
SPEC	specification	T.D.	towel dispenser
SPECS	specifications	T.G.	tempered glass
SPKR	speaker	T.O.	top of
SQ	square	T.O.C.	top of curb

SQ.IN.	square inch	T.O.M.	top of masonry
ST	street	T.O.W.	top of wall
ST.PART.	steel partition	T.P.	top of pavement
ST.STL.	stainless steel	T.P.D.	toilet paper
ST.S.	storm sewer		dispenser
STA	station	T.S.	towel strip
STAG	staggered	T.S.	tube steel
STC	sound transmission	T.V.	television
	class	TANG	tangent
STD	standard	TECH	technical
STER	sterilizer	TECHS	technicians
STIFF	stiffener	TEL	telephone
STIR	stirrup	TEMP	temperature
STL	steel	TEMP	tempered
STOR	storage	TEMP	template
STOR.CL.	storage closet	TEMP	temporary
STR	structural	TERM	terminate
STR	structure	TERR	terrace

STRIPG	stripping	TERR	terrazzo
SUB	substitute	THD	thread
SUP	supply	THK	thick
SUP	support	THK	thickness
SUPP	supplement	THR	threshold
SUPT	superintendent	THRU	through
SUR	surface	TLT	toilet
SUSP	suspend	TRANS	transformer
SUSP	suspended	TRTMNT	treatment
SUSP.CLG.	suspended ceiling	TSTAT	thermostat
SW	switch	TYP	typical
U.H.	unit heater	VIN	vinyl
U.N.O.	unless noted otherwise	VIT	vitreous
		VOL	volume
U.O.N.	unless otherwise noted	W	water
		W	west
U.S.	utility shelf	W	wide
UC	undercut	W.CAB.	wall cabinet

UG	underground	W.GL.	wire glass
UL	underwriters	W.C.	water closet
	laboratories, inc.	W.F.	wide flange
ULT	ultimate	W.H.	wall hydrant
UNEX	unexcavated	W.H.	water heater
UNF	unfinished	W.L.	water line
UR	urinal	W.R.	water-resistant
V	valve	W.S.	weather stripping
V	volt	W.T.W	wall to wall
V.A.T.	vinyl asbestos tile	W.W. F	welded wire fabric
V.B.	valve box	W.W.M.	welded wire mesh
V.B.	vapor barrier	W/	with
V.B.	vinyl base	W/O	without
V.C.P.	vitrified clay pipe	WD	wood
V.C.T.	vinyl composition	WH.C.	wheel chair
	tile	WHSE	warehouse
V.I.F.	verify in field	WNDW	window
V.T.R.	vent through roof	WP	waterproof

V.W.C.	vinyl wall covering	WP	waterproofing
VAC	vacuum	WP	weatherproof
VAR	variable	WP	weatherproofing
VAR	varies	WSCT	wainscot
VAR	varnish	WT	weight
VENT	ventilate	X	by (as 6*8)
VENT	ventilation	Y.P.	yield point
VENT	ventilator	Y.S.	yield strength
VENT	vertical	YD	yard
VEST	vestibule	Z	zone

Appendix 2.   Common Terms in Architecture

First floor – Usually on top of the ground floor

Second floor – A floor above the first floor

One storey – A building having two floors (UK). A building having one floor (U.S).

2 storey – A building having three floors (UK). A building having two floors (U.S).

Bungalow – A single-storey building.

Basement floor – This is any floor below the ground floor.

Ground floor – It is a floor directly on top of the ground level.

Ground Level – The point at the level of the topsoil.

Mezzanine floor – This is a floor in-between two floors, smaller than the typical floor.

Penthouse – A room or space above the major roof.

Attic – This is the room or space in the roof. The space between the ceiling frame of the topmost storey and the underside of the roof framing.

Duplex – A single two or more floor structure.

Semi-detached house – Two or more buildings sharing a common wall.

Skyscraper – A structure that is going up so high. A very tall multi-storey building.

Corridor – A circulation space in a building.

Veranda – External opening in a building created within the frame of the structure to appreciate the environment or as a shading device.

Balcony – External projection in the building resembling the verandah.

Lobby – A space at the entrance of a building, usually deep and sometimes allowing for other complementary activities to go on, e.g. A.T.M space in a mall.

Passage – A space connecting one room to another, usually a narrow rectangular space.

Sit-Out – A space projecting out of a building larger than a balcony which can house settee in -the -round and other furniture.

Entrance foyer – A large open space acting as the ushering space to a building, hotel, theatre or any structure.

Entrance vestibule - A room between the side door and the main part of a building or house.

Entrance porch – An entry space into a building looking more like a square.

Entrance Corridor – An entry space into a building with a rectangular outlook.

Aisle – A rigid or flexible pathway defined by pews or columns usually very long and primarily for circulation.

Recess - A niche, alcove or a smaller unit.

Niche – A recess in a wall, (rectilinear, circular, or oval) smaller than an alcove covered with a dome or lean-to-roof used for housing sculpture and relief work especially in an ecclesiastic building.

Terrace – A space on the roof or ground floor level that can accommodate activity for a larger number of people than the foyer.

Courtyard – An open area that is partially or fully enclosed by walls or piers.

Atrium – A large vertical space, most time located at the centre that opens to three or more floors with sky lighting at the zenith.

Void – An opening or space not floored, existing in space within a building.

Canopy – A hood above a niche, entrance, pulpit projecting on its own supported by posts and lintels.

Danpalon – A light material bolted to a steel structure usually under tension covering an entrance, carport and its like.

Rotunda – A circular building covered usually with a dome, cone or cupolas.

Concourse - Large corridor space in a public building such as an airport or train station where people gather in or pass-through

Awning – A sheet of fabric hung above a window or door as a protection against rain and sun especially outside a shop.

Room – A place in a house where an activity can take place

Suite – A connected group of rooms with different functions designed to function as a unit e.g. a hotel suite.

Cloakroom – A space at the entrance of a room used for hanging clothes. A room for the deposit and checking of outer clothes

Restroom – Convenience or toilet area

Living room – A room in residential or public buildings for housing and entertaining visitors

Kitchen – A room used for preparing and cooking of food, often where meals are also kept and eaten.

Kitchenette – A smaller kitchen

Store – A room in a house for keeping wanted and unwanted items.

Pantry – A store for putting only food items.

Ante-room – A room adjacent to a large and more important room, usually ushering into the large room.

Landing – A stair landing on a floor

Platform - A stair landing between two floors.

Stair or Elevator core – A vertical space extending to the roof where the stair is located

Duct – Any space (vertical or horizontal) used to house services in a building.

Service floor – A full-floor usually with a lower headroom provided to house all the services and utilities in a building.

Service duct – A space (circular, rectilinear, oval or polygon) either conduit or surface provided to house electrical and mechanical services in a building.

Service lift or stair –Usually provided for members of staff, as in a hotel

Attic – A space or room at the top of a building under the roof often used for storing.

Dormer window – Windows sticking out from a sloping roof

Alcove – A small space in a room formed by one part of the wall being further back than the parts on each side.

Arcade – A covered area or passage joined to a building on one side with columns

Arch-way – An entrance or passage formed by an arch

Ancillary – Providing support or help. Additional or extra space or unit or department

Manhole – A covered opening in a street that provides access for cleaning and repair works on town services.

Septic tank – A storage tank below the ground level that receives the whole discharge of sewage from the building sewer, separate solid from liquid, store digested solid and allows the liquid to be discharged to the soakaway pit

Soak away – A pit excavated in the earth's surface which receives excess surface water and allows it to drain gradually into the soil.

Inspection Chamber – A shallow manhole connecting two or more drain pipes at an angle.

Colonnade – A row of columns as in an orthodox church

Order – Classical name for columns developed at the early times by the Greeks e.g. Doric, Ionic, Tuscan and Composite.

Cornice – A molded projection that crowns or finishes the part to which it is affixed.

Clerestory – An upper part of a wall pierced by windows that helps to admit light and air.

Stanchions – A vertical pole, pillar, or beam usually made of steel and exposed giving support to a slab or roof.

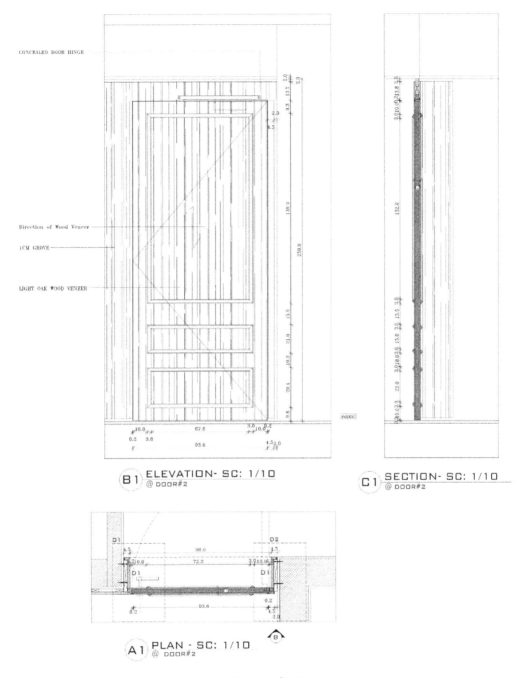

CONCEALED DOOR HINGE

Direction of Wood Veneer

1CM GROVE

LIGHT OAK WOOD VENEER

B1 ELEVATION- SC: 1/10
@ DOOR#2

C1 SECTION- SC: 1/10
@ DOOR#2

A1 PLAN - SC: 1/10
@ DOOR#2

Appendix 1

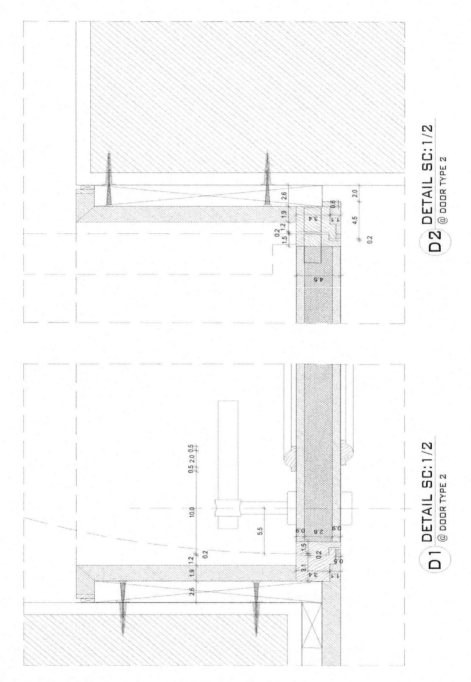

D2 DETAIL SC:1/2
@ DOOR TYPE 2

D1 DETAIL SC:1/2
@ DOOR TYPE 2

Appendix 2

202

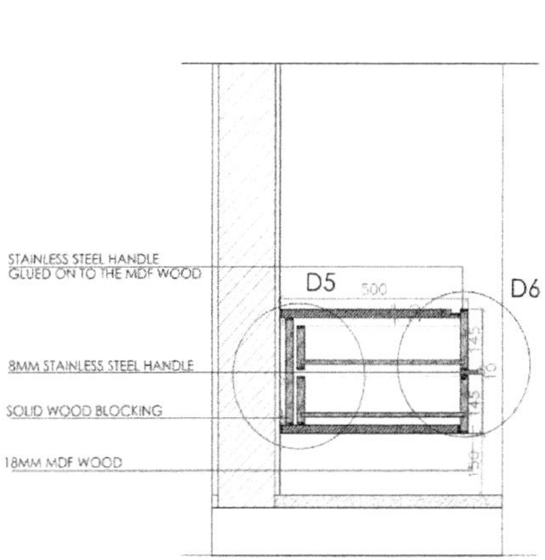

STAINLESS STEEL HANDLE
GLUED ON TO THE MDF WOOD
8MM STAINLESS STEEL HANDLE
SOLID WOOD BLOCKING
18MM MDF WOOD
D5
D6
500

C SECTION- SC: -
@ BATHROOM CABINET

B
8MM STAINLESS STEEL
STRIP DRAWER HANDLE
18 MM MDF WOOD VENEER
100
1500
100
565
465
150
150
150
145
145

B ELEVATION - SC: -
@ BATHROOM CABINET

D1
D2
D3
D4
529
468
468
540
529
405
405
558
558
558
1680
B

A PLAN - SC: -
@ BATHROOM CABINET

Appendix 2A

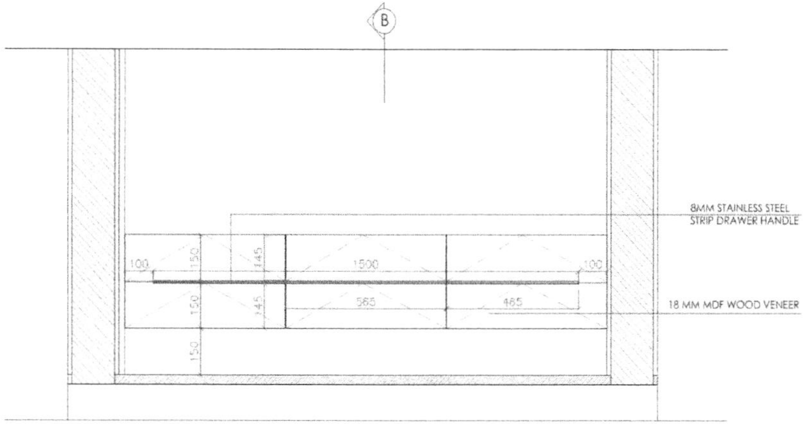

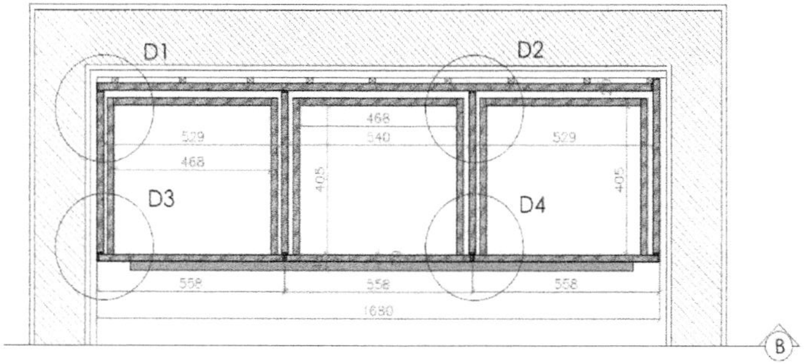

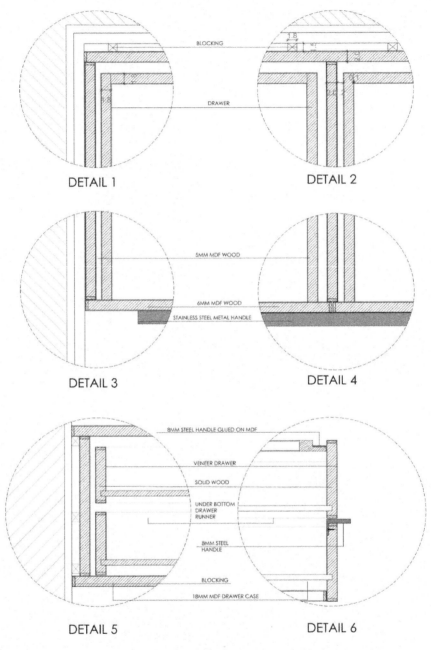

DETAIL 1

DETAIL 2

DETAIL 3

DETAIL 4

DETAIL 5

DETAIL 6

Appendix 2B

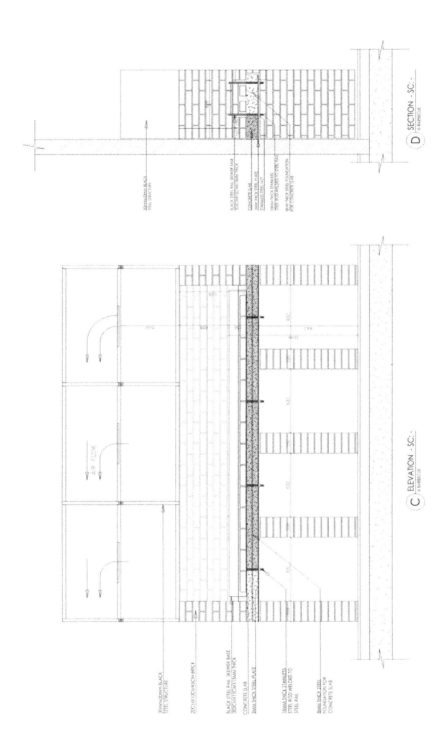

Appendix 3A

205

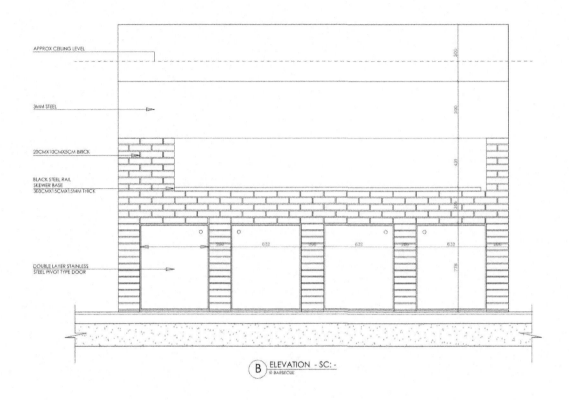

APPROX CEILING LEVEL

3MM STEEL

20CMX10CMX5CM BRICK

BLACK STEEL RAIL
SKEWER BASE
303CMX15CMX15MM THICK

DOUBLE LAYER STAINLESS
STEEL PIVOT TYPE DOOR

B ELEVATION - SC: -
@ BARBECUE

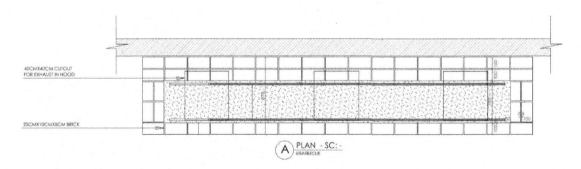

40CMX40CM CUTOUT
FOR EXHAUST IN HOOD

20CMX10CMX5CM BRICK

A PLAN - SC: -
@ BARBECUE

Appendix 3B

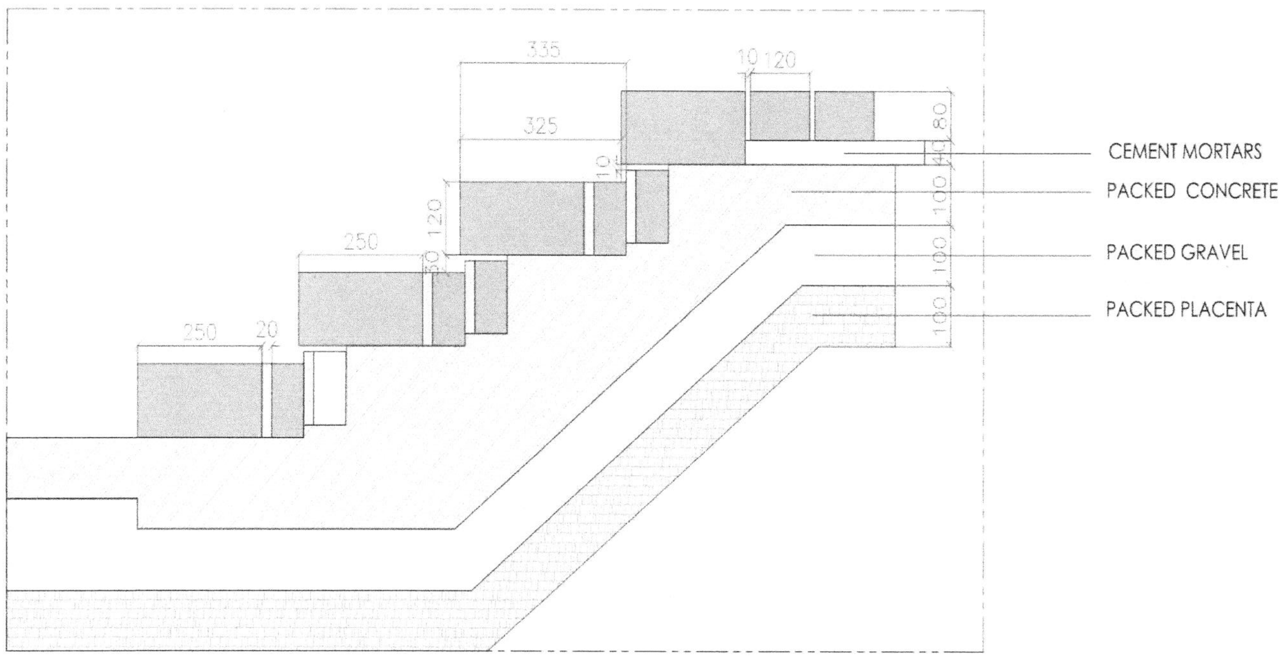

CEMENT MORTARS
PACKED CONCRETE
PACKED GRAVEL
PACKED PLACENTA

80 40 100 40 100 100 100

10 20

10

335

325

10

50 120

120

250

20

250

A STAIRS- SC:-
@ PATIO STAIRS

Appendix 4

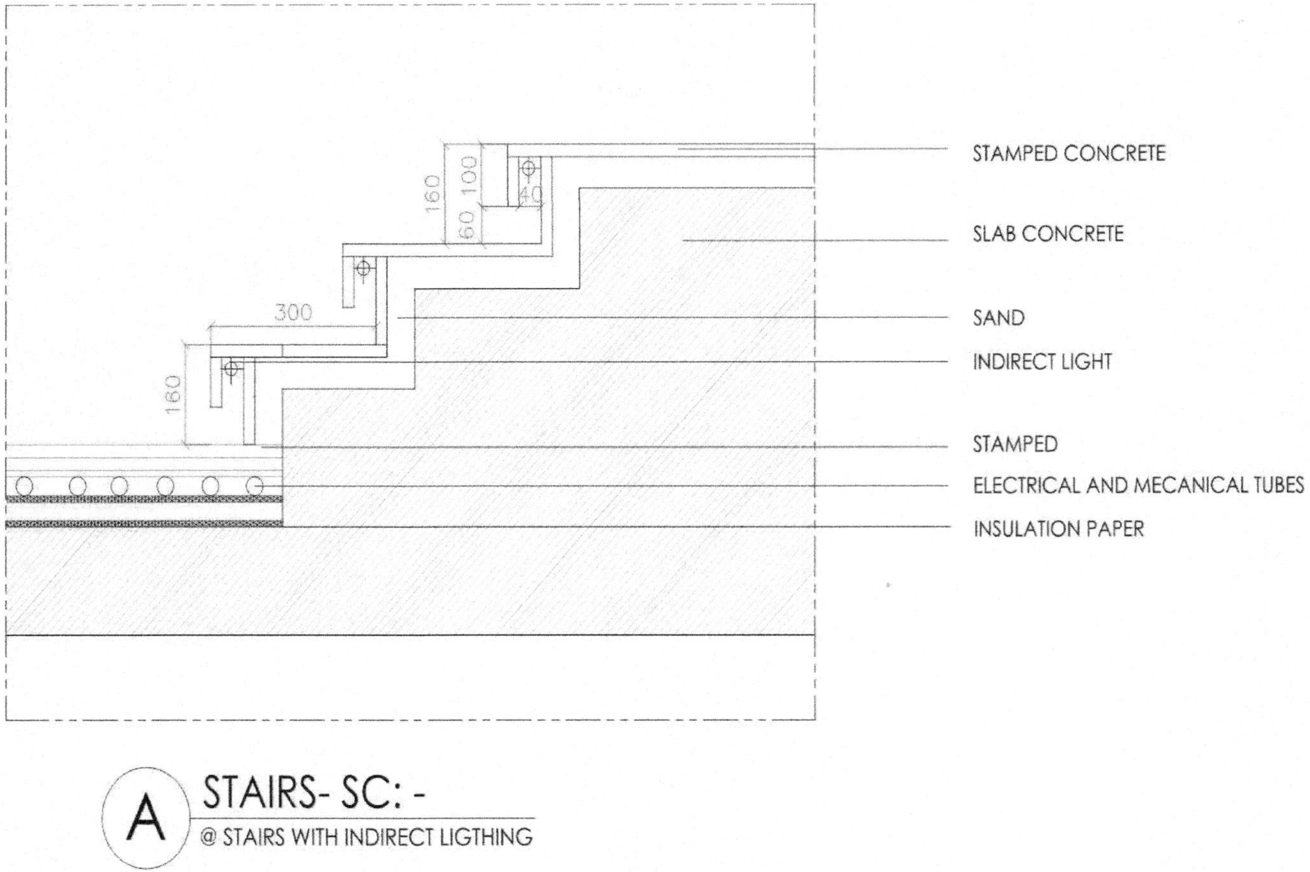

STAMPED CONCRETE

SLAB CONCRETE

SAND

INDIRECT LIGHT

STAMPED

ELECTRICAL AND MECANICAL TUBES

INSULATION PAPER

160
100
60
40

300

160

A STAIRS- SC: -
@ STAIRS WITH INDIRECT LIGTHING

Appendix 5

208

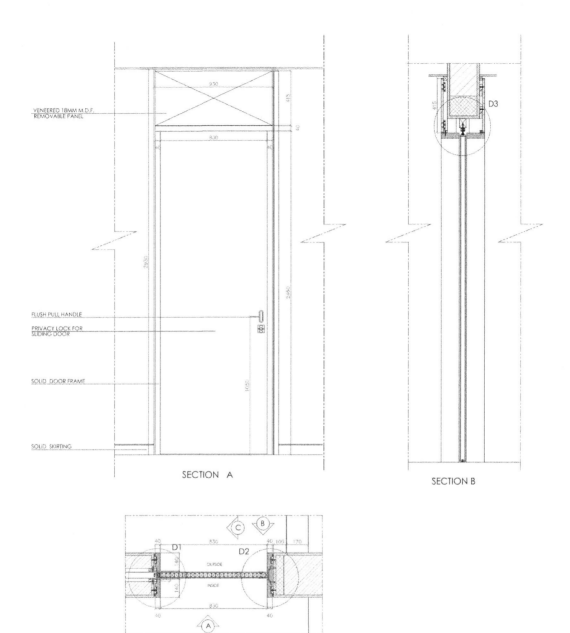

VENEERED 18MM M.D.F.
REMOVABLE PANEL

FLUSH PULL HANDLE

PRIVACY LOCK FOR
SLIDING DOOR

SOLID DOOR FRAME

SOLID SKIRTING

SECTION A

SECTION B

D3

D1   D2

OUTSIDE

INSIDE

PLAN VIEW

Appendix 6

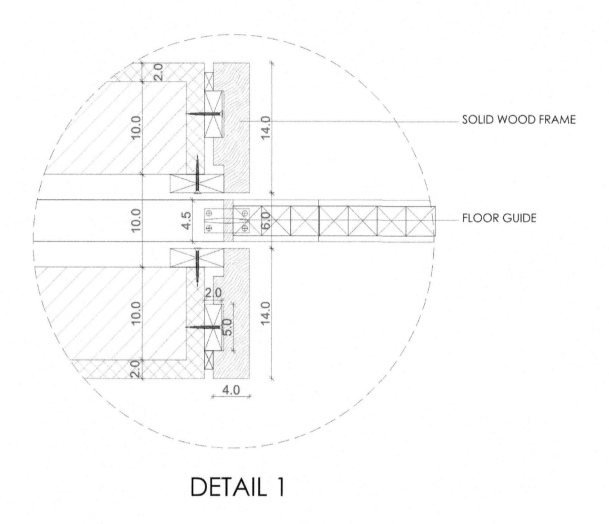

SOLID WOOD FRAME

FLOOR GUIDE

DETAIL 1

Appendix 6A

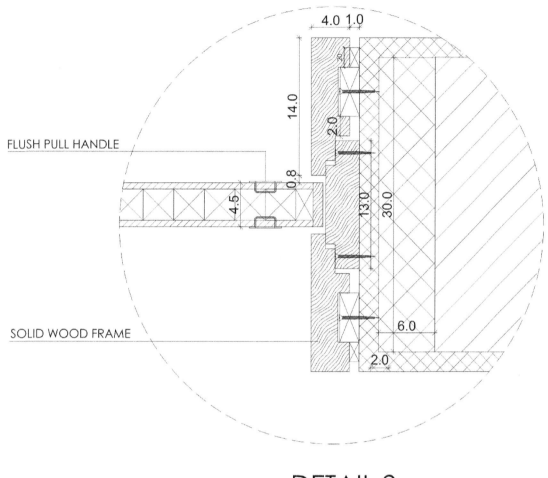

FLUSH PULL HANDLE

SOLID WOOD FRAME

DETAIL 2

Appendix 6B

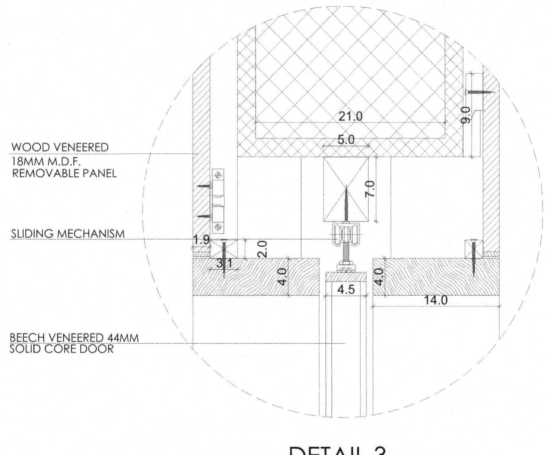

WOOD VENEERED
18MM M.D.F.
REMOVABLE PANEL

SLIDING MECHANISM

BEECH VENEERED 44MM
SOLID CORE DOOR

21.0

5.0

9.0

7.0

1.9

2.0

3.1

4.0

4.5

4.0

14.0

DETAIL 3

Appendix 6C

REFERENCES

Booker, P, (1963) *History of engineering drawing* (London: Chatto and Windus.)

Camerota, F. 2004. Renaissance descriptive geometry. The codification of drawing methods. In Picturing Machines 1400–1700, edited by W. Lefèvre. Cambridge, MA: MIT Press, 175–208.

Ching, F. D. K. (2011). *Architectural Graphics*. Hoboken: John Wiley & Sons.

Gieseke, F.E., et al.(1974: Technical Drawing, 6th ed., New York. The MacMillan Co.,

Harvey, J. (1972). *The mediaeval architect*. London: Wayland

Henninger-Voss, M. (2004) Measures of Success: Military Engineering and the Architectonic Understanding of Design. Mit Press.

Mayer, R. (1940). The Artists Handbook of Materials and Techniques, Viking, 1940, ISBN 978-0670837014

Parsons, W. B. (1968). Engineers and Engineering in the Renaissance. Cambridge, MA: MIT Press.

Shelby, L.R. (1964) The Role of the Master Mason in Medieval English Building. _Speculum _39(3):387-403

Shelby, L.R. (1972). The Geometrical Knowledge of Mediaeval Master Masons. _ Speculum_ 47(3):395-421

Thomas, M.L (1978). Architectural Working Drawings; A Professional Technique. New York. McGraw-Hill Book.

Vitruvius, P., & Morgan, M. H. (1960). *Vitruvius: The ten books on architecture*. New York: Dover Publications.

ABOUT THE BOOK

Working drawings, though a subset, of the design process, yet, a very important aspect of it. Thus, architects must develop good design vocabularies in order to achieve excellent results. Strict adherence to design rules and conventions will reduce the ambiguity created in most working drawings and enable architects speak similar language over a period of time, thus creating a clearer pathway for other allied professionals to follow.

This book on the working drawing will help to relay some of the dos and don'ts in drafting working drawings. It is good for practicing architects, those studying architecture or related courses, allied professionals and scholars. It affords the reader the opportunity to reflect on the symbols, signs, explanations, terminologies that are likely to come up when preparing working drawings. It also takes into consideration first-timers who have little or no experience in drafting skills as it starts from the rudimentary, and takes the reader all the way through, to the professional requirements.

Printed in Great Britain
by Amazon

37393221R20119